THE

HISTORY

OF THE

LATE WAR

BETWEEN THE UNITED STATES AND
GREAT BRITAIN.

Published by Left of Brain Books

Copyright © 2021 Left of Brain Books

ISBN 978-1-396-32114-6

First Edition

All rights reserved. No part of this publication may be reproduced, distributed, or transmitted in any form or by any means, including photocopying, recording, or other electronic or mechanical methods, without the prior written permission of the publisher, except in the case of brief quotations embodied in critical reviews and certain other noncommercial uses permitted by copyright law. Left of Brain Books is a division of Left of Brain Onboarding Pty Ltd.

Table of Contents

CHAP. I.   1
President's message—causes of the war—energetic measures proposed.   1

CHAP. II.   4
Report of the Committee—Declaration of war.   4

CHAP. III.   6
Reception of the Declaration of war in Great Britain—her friends in America—Caleb strong—Hartford Convention.   6

CHAP. IV.   11
John Henry—Elijah Parish.   11

CHAP. V.   13
American Army—Militia—Navy—-British Navy—Rogers' First Cruise—capture Of the U. S. Brig Nautilus—removal of aliens beyond tide-water.   13

CHAP. VI.   16
Hull's expedition—he enters Canada, and encamps at Sandwich—issues his Proclamation—retreats to Detroit.   16

CHAP. VII.   19
Hull's expedition—surrender of his army and the whole Michigan territory—his trial and pardon by the President—capture of Michilimackinack.   19

CHAP. VIII.   25
Capture of the British frigate Guerriere, by the united states' frigate constitution, captain hull—capture of the Alert Sloop of war, by the Essex, Captain Porter.   25

CHAP. IX.   28
Attack on Sackett's Harbor—affair of Ogdensburgh—British drove from St. Regis, by the Troy militia under major young— the brigs Adams and Caledonia re-captured by Capt. Elliot, near fort Erie.   28

CHAP. X.   31
Battle of Queenstown—the British General Brock killed.   31

CHAP. XI. 34

Gen. Smyth Succeeds Gen. Van Rensselaer— his Attempt to Cross the Niagara, And Failure —causes. 34

CHAP. XII. 36

Capture of the sloop of war Frolic, of 22 guns, by the United States' sloop of war wasp, of 18 guns. 36

CHAP. XIII. 38

Capture of the British frigate Macedonian, by Com. Decatur, in the frigate United States —brig vixen captured by the British frigate Southampton. 38

CHAP. XIV. 42

Affairs in the north—skirmishes—battle of Frenchtown, on the river Raisin— capture of Gen. Winchester's army—massacre of American prisoners. 42

CHAP. XV. 47

Capture of the British Frigate java, by the United States frigate Constitution. 47

CHAP. XVI. 51

Com. Rogers' return from a second cruise— capture of the United States' brig Viper—the general Armstrong and a British frigate—privateering. 51

CHAP. XVII. 55

Capture and burning of Ogdensburgh by the British. 55

CHAP. XVIII. 57

Capture of the Peacock, of 18 guns, by the U. S. Sloop of war hornet, of 16 guns—return of the Chesapeake from a cruise. 57

CHAP. XIX. 61

Capture of Little York, in Upper Canada— the destruction of the whole American army prevented by the precaution of Gen. Pike— his death. 61

CHAP. XX. 68

Sketches of the History of America. 68

CHAP. XXI. 72

Depredations in the Chesapeake—Havre-de-Grace burnt by the British under Adm. Cockburn—attack on Crany Island—Hampton taken by the British—Outrages. 72

CHAP. XXII. 78

Russian mediation—Bayard and Gallatin sail for St. Petersburgh—the British compelled to abandon the siege of Fort Meigs. 78

CHAP XXIII. 80

Surrender of Fort George and Fort Erie to the Americans—gen. Brown drives the British from before Sackett's Harbor, with great loss—Gens. Winder and Chandler made prisoners at Forty-mile creek. 80

CHAP. XXIV. 83

Capture of the Chesapeake—Com. Decatur blockaded in New-London. 83

CHAP. XXV. 88

Capture of Col. Boerstler and Major Chapin, with their command—treatment of prisoners—Major Chapin's escape. 88

CHAP. XXVI. 90

Capture of Fort Schlosser and Black Rock— Gen. Dearborn resigns his command to gen. Boyd) on account of sickness—six nations declare war against Canada. 90

CHAP. XXVII. 93

Affairs on Lake Ontario, between the fleets of Com. Chauncey and Sir James Yeo. 93

CHAP. XXVIII. 95

Affairs on Lake Champlain—pillage of Plattsburgh by the British—bombardment of Burlington—depredations committed in the Chesapeake, and along the coast. 95

CHAP. XXIX. 98

Major Croghan defeats the British and Indians, under Gen. Proctor, in their attack on fort Stephenson, Lower Sandusky. 98

CHAP. XXX. 101

British Schooner Dominica; of 14 Guns, Captured by the privateer Decatur, Of 7 Guns— U. S. brig Argus captured by the Pelican— capture of the Boxer by the U. S. brig Enterprise, 101

CHAP. XXXI. 105

The capture of the British Fleet on Lake Erie, by the American fleet under Com. Perry. 105

CHAP. XXXII. 109

Capture of Malden and Detroit—the army of Gen. Proctor retreat towards the Moravian towns—Gen. Harrison pursues them. 109

CHAP. XXXIII. 113

Battle of the Thames—Gen. Harrison captures the British army under Gen. Proctor—illuminations on account of it—news of it received in England. 113

CHAP. XXXIV. 117

War with the creek nation of Indians—massacre of fort Mimms—Georgia and Tennessee militia, under General Jackson, retaliate. 117

CHAP. XXXV. 120

Continuation of the war with the Creeks—Gen. Jackson's grand victory over them—they sue for peace—a treaty is concluded with them. 120

CHAP. XXXVI. 125

Plan of attack on Montreal defeated. 125

CHAP. XXXVII. 129

Newark burnt—Fort George evacuated—Niagara frontier laid Waste— Buffalo burnt. 129

CHAP. XXXVIII. 131

Cruise of the U. S. Frigate Essex, D. Porter, commander—her defence and capture, at Valparaiso. 131

CHAP. XXXIX. 136

Capture of the u. S. Sloop of War Frolic, the British frigate Orpheus—capture of the British sloop of war L'Epervier, by the Peacock, Capt. Warrington— capture of the Reindeer, by the Wasp, Capt. Blakely—the Avon captured and sunk— U. S. Vessels Syren and rattlesnake captured—Admiral Cochrane declares the whole American coast in a state of blockade. 136

CHAP. XL. 139

Breaking up of the cantonment at French Mills—affair at La Cole mill—Major Appling captures two hundred British seamen —Gen. Brown captures Fort Erie—battle of Chippawa plains. 139

CHAP. XLI. 143

Battle of Bridgewater. 143

CHAP. XLII. 146

Assault on Fort Erie, by the British, under Gen. Drummond—Gen. Brown resumes his command—sallies out of Fort Erie against the British camp—MacArthur's expedition into Canada. 146

CHAP. XLIII. 150

Attack on Stonington, by the British ships of war, which are defeated and driven off. 150

CHAP. XLIV. 152

Affairs in the Chesapeake—British army move up the Patuxent—land and march towards the city of Washington—prepare themselves for battle at Bladensburgh. 152

CHAP. XLV. 155

Capture of Washington—sacking of Alexandria—death of Sir Peter Parker. 155

CHAP. XLVI. 162

British, under Gov. Prevost, go against Plattsburgh—Com. Macdonough captures the British squadron on Lake Champlain. 162

CHAP. XLVII. 166

Battle of Plattsburgh—defeat Of Sir George Prevost. 166

CHAP. XLVIII. 169

Attack on Baltimore, by the British army, under Gen. Ross, and the fleet under Admirals Cochrane and Cockburn. 169

CHAP. XLIX. 174

Destruction of the privateer gen. Armstrong, Samuel C. Reid, Captain—Scorpion and Tigress captured— U. S. frigate Adams burnt —Castine—Fort Boyer attacked—destruction of the pirates at Barrataria, by Com. Patterson—Gen. Jackson captures Pensacola, and returns to New-Orleans. 174

CHAP. L. 180

Steam-boats—Fulton—torpedoes—attempt to blow up the Plantagenet—kidnapping Joshua Penny. 180

CHAP. LI. 185

Affairs in and about New-York, the first commercial city in America—working on the fortifications of Brooklyn and Haerlem— capture of the British tender eagle, by the Yankee smack. 185

CHAP. LII. 191

Affairs on the ocean—privateer Prince of Neufchatel—Marquis of Tweedale defeated in Upper Canada—capture of the President —loss of the Sylph—capture of the Cyane and the Levant by the Constitution—capture of the St. Lawrence—capture of the Penguin by the Hornet, Captain Biddle. 191

CHAP. LIII. 195

British fleet arrives near New-Orleans—the American flotilla captured—attacks by the British upon the army of Gen. Jackson. 195

CHAP. LIV. 199

Grand Battle of New-Orleans. 199

CHAP. LV. 204

Peace. 204

ALGERINE WAR. 208

American squadron sails from New-York—arrives on the Mediterranean, and captures the Algerine vessels—treaty of peace with the Dey—affairs at Tunis and Tripoli—Decatur's return to America. 208

CONCLUSION. 214

Commodore Bainbridge—Lord Exmouth's Expedition against Algiers. 214

BIBLE SOCIETIES AND SUNDAY SCHOOLS 216

COMMERCIAL TREATY.	220
DECATUR'S TREATY	226
ARTICLES OF AGREEMENT.	233

CHAP. I.

President's message—causes of the war—energetic measures proposed.

Now it came to pass, in the one thousand eight hundred and twelfth year of the christian era, and in the thirty and sixth year after the people of the provinces of Columbia had declared themselves independent of all the kingdoms of the earth;

That in the sixth month of the same year, on the first day of the month, the chief Governor, whom the people had chosen to rule over the land of Columbia;

Even *James*, whose sur-name was MADISON, delivered a written paper[1] to the GREAT SANHEDRIM[2] of the people, who were assembled together.

And the name of the city where the people were gathered together was called after the name of the chief captain of the land of Columbia, whose fame extendeth to the uttermost parts of the earth: albeit, he had gone to the land of his fathers.

Nevertheless, the people loved him, inasmuch as he wrought their deliverance from the yoke of tyranny in times past: so they called the city WASHINGTON.

Now, when the written paper was received, the doors of the chambers of the Great Sanhedrim were closed, and a seal was put upon every man's mouth.

---

[1] President's manifesto.
[2] Congress

And the counsellors of the nation, and the wise men thereof, ordered the written paper which James had delivered unto them to be read aloud; and the interpretation thereof was in this wise:

Lo! the lords and the princes of the Kingdom of Britain, in the fulness of their altar of Liberty, and violated the sanctuary thereof:

Inasmuch as they hearkened not unto the voice of moderation, when the voice of the people of Columbia was, Peace! peace!

Inasmuch as they permitted not the tall ships of Columbia to sail in peace on the waters of the mighty deep; saying in their hearts, These spoils shall be given unto the king.

Inasmuch as they robbed the ships of Columbia of the strong men that wrought therein, and used them for their own use, even as a man useth his ox or his ass.

Inasmuch as they kept the men stolen from the ships of Columbia in bondage many years, and caused them to fight the battles of the king, even against their own brethren! neither gave they unto them silver or gold, but many stripes.

Now the men of Columbia were not like unto the slaves of Britain; neither were their backs hardened unto the whip, as were the servants of the king; therefore they murmured, and their murmurings have been heard.

Moreover the Council of Britain sent forth a Decree to all the nations of the earth, sealed with the signet of the Prince Regent, who governed the nation in the name of the King his father; for, lo! the King was possessed of an evil spirit, and his son reigned in his stead.

For the lords of the kingdom of Britain loved to dwell under the shadow of George the King, and under the shadow of George his son.

16 Now this Decree of the Council of Britain was a grievous thing, inasmuch as it permitted not those who dealt in merchandize to go whithersoever they chose, and trade freely with all parts of the earth.

And it fell hard upon the people Of Columbia; for the king said unto them, Ye shall come unto me and pay tribute, then may ye depart to another country.

Now these things pleased the pirates and the cruisers and all the sea-robbers of Britain mightily, inasmuch as they could rob with impunity the commerce of Columbia, under the cloak of British honor.

Furthermore, have not the servants of the king leagued with the savages of the wilderness, and given unto them silver and gold, and placed the destroying engines in their hands?

Thereby stirring up the spirit of Satan within them, that they might spill the blood of the people of Columbia; even the blood of our old men, our wives, and our little ones!

Thus hath Britain in her heart commenced War against the people of Columbia, whilst they have cried aloud for peace: and when she smote them on the one cheek they have turned unto her the other also.

Now, therefore, shall we the independent people of Columbia, sit down silently, as slaves, and bow the neck to Britain?

Or, shall we nobly, and like our forefathers, assert our rights, and defend that which the Lord hath given unto us, LIBERTY and INDEPENDENCE?

CHAP. II.

Report of the Committee—Declaration of war.

Now, when there was an end made of reading the paper which James had written, the Sanhedrim communed one with another touching the matter.

And they chose certain wise men from among them to deliberate thereon.

And they commanded them to go forth from their presence, for that purpose, and return again on the third day of the same month.

Now, when the third day arrived, at the eleventh hour of the day, they came forth and presented themselves before the Great Sanhedrim of the people.

And the chief of the wise men, whom they had chosen, opened his mouth and spake unto them after this manner:

Behold! day and night have we meditated upon the words which James hath delivered, and we are weary withal, for our hearts wished peace.

But the wickedness of the kingdom of Great Britain, and the cruelty of the princes thereof, towards the peaceable inhabitants of the land of Columbia, may be likened unto the fierce lion, when he putteth his paw upon the innocent lamb to devour him.

Nevertheless, the lamb shall not be slain; for the Lord will be his deliverer.

And if, peradventure, the people of Columbia go not out to battle against the king, then will the manifold wrongs committed against them be increased ten-fold, and they shall be as a mock and a bye-word among all nations.

Moreover, the righteousness of your cause shall lead you to glory, and the pillars of your liberty shall not be shaken.

Therefore, say we unto you, Gird on your swords and go forth to battle against the king; even against the strong powers of Britain; and the Lord God of Hosts be with you.

Now when the great Sanhedrim of the people heard those things which the wise men had uttered, they pondered them in their minds many days, and weighed them well.

Even until the seventeenth day of the month pondered they in secret concerning the matter.

And it was so, that on the next day they sent forth a Decree, making WAR upon the kingdom of Great Britain, and upon the servants and upon the slaves thereof.

And the Decree was signed with the hand writing of James, the chief Governor of the land of Columbia.

After these things, the doors of the chambers of the Sanhedrim were opened.

CHAP. III.

Reception of the Declaration of war in Great Britain—her friends in America—Caleb strong—Hartford Convention.

And it came to pass, that when the princes and the lords and the counsellors of Britain saw the Decree, their wrath was kindled, and their hearts were ready to burst with indignation.

For, verily, said they, this insult bath overflowed the cup of our patience; and now will we chastise the impudence of these Yankees, and the people of Columbia shall bow before the king.

(Now the word Yankees was used by the people of Britain as a term of reproach.)

Then will we rule them with a rod of iron; and they shall be, unto us, hewers of wood and drawers of water.

For, verily, shall we suffer these cunning Yankees to beard the mighty lion, with half a dozen fir-built frigates, the men whereof are but mercenary cowards, bastards and outlaws?

Neither durst they array themselves in battle against the men of Britain; no! we will sweep their stars from the face of the waters, and their name shall be heard no more among nations.

Shall the proud conquerors of Europe not laugh to scorn the feeble efforts of a few unorganized soldiers, undisciplined, and fresh from the plough, the hoe, and the mattock?

Yea, they shall surely fall; for they were not bred to fighting as were the servants of the king.

Their large cities, their towns, and their villages will we burn with consuming fire.

Their oil, and their wheat, and their rye, and their corn, and their barley, and their rice, and their buckwheat, and their oats, and their flax, and all the products of their country will we destroy, and scatter the remnants thereof to the four winds of heaven.

All these things, and more, will we do unto this froward people. 12 Neither shall there be found safety for age or sex from the destroying swords of the soldiers of the king.

Neither shall there be found safety for age or sex from the destroying swords of the soldiers of the king.

Save in those provinces and towns where dwell the friends of the king; for lo! said they, the king's friends are many.

These will we spare; neither will we hurt a hair of their heads: nor shall the savages of the wilderness stain the scalping knife or the tomahawk with the blood of the king's friends.

Now it happened about this time that there were numbers of the inhabitants of the country of Columbia whose hearts yearned after the king of Britain.

These men were called Tories, which signifieth, in the vernacular tongue, the blind followers of royalty.

And with their false flattering words they led astray some of the children of COLUMBIAN LIBERTY; for their tongues were smoother than oil.

Evil machinations entered into their hearts, and the poison of their breath might be likened unto the deadly Bohon Upas, which rears its lofty branches in the barren valley of Java.³

And they strove to dishearten the true friends of the great Sanhedrim; but they prevailed not.

Moreover, Satan entered into the heart of one of the governors of the east, and he was led astray by the wickedness thereof, even Caleb, the shittamite.⁴

Now Caleb, which in the Cherokee tongue, signifieth an ass, liked not the decree of the great Sanhedrim, inasmuch as he favored the king of Britain; and, though willing to become a beast of burden, yet would not move on account of his very great stupidity.

And he said unto the captains of the hosts of the state over which he presided, Lo! it seemeth not meet unto me that ye go forth to battle against the king.

For, lo! are not the fighting men of Britain in multitude as the sand on the sea shore? and shall we prevail against them?

Are not the mighty ships of the king spread over the whole face of the waters? is not Britain the "bulwark of our religion?"

Therefore, I command that ye go not out to battle, but every man remain in his own house.

And all the governors of the east listened unto the voice of Caleb, the shittamite.

---

³ Of the existence of this wonderful tree there have been doubts: but the reader is referred to the relation of P.N. Foersch, who has given a satisfactory account of it, from his own travels in its neighborhood.

⁴ Shittamite, in the hebrew, is applied to a dissenter: perhaps it may be equally applicable here.

Moreover, the angel of the Lord whispered in the ear of Caleb, and spake unto him, saying,

If, peradventure, thou dost refuse to obey the laws of the land, the thing will not be pleasant in the sight of the Lord;

Inasmuch as it may cause the people to rise up one against another, and spill the blood of their own children.

And the time of warfare will be lengthened out, and the blood of thousands will be upon thine head.

And Satan spake, and said unto Caleb, Fear not; for if thou wilt forsake thy country, and throw off the paltry subterfuge of COLUMBIAN LIBERTY, and defy the councils of the great Sanhedrim,

Then shall thy name be proclaimed with the sound of the trumpet throughout all the earth; and thou shalt be a prince and a ruler over this people.

Now the smooth words of Satan tickled Caleb mightily, and he hearkened unto the counsel of the wicked one:

For the good counsel given unto him was as water thrown upon a rock.

But when the chief governor and the great Sanhedrim of the people saw the wickedness of Caleb, their hearts were moved with pity toward him and his followers: yea, even those who had made a convention at the little town of *Hartford*.

Neither doth the scribe desire to dwell upon the wickedness which came into the village of Hartford, the signification of the name whereof, in the vernacular tongue, appeareth not.

For the meddling therewith is as the green pool of unclean waters, when a man casteth a stone therein.

CHAP. IV.

John Henry—Elijah Parish.

Let the children of Columbia beware of false prophets, which come in sheep's clothing; for it is written, Ye shall know them by their fruits.

Now it came to pass, that a certain man, whose sir-name was *Henry*, came before James, the chief governor, and opened his mouth, and spake unto him, saying,

Lo! if thou wilt give unto me two score and ten thousand pieces of silver, then will I unfold unto thee the witchcraft of Britain, that thereby thy nation may not be caught in her snares.

And James said unto him, Verily, for the good of my country, I will do this thing.

And immediately the man Henry opened his mouth, a second time, and said,

Lo! the lords and the counsellors of Britain have made a covenant with me, and have promised me many pieces of gold if I would make a league with the provinces of the east, that they might favor the king; and long and faithfully have I labored in their cause.

But they deceived me, even as they would deceive the people of Columbia; for their promises are as the idle wind that passeth by, which no man regardeth.

And, when he had gotten the silver into his own hands, he departed to the land of the *Gauls*, where he remaineth even until this day.

Nevertheless, the people profited much thereby; inasmuch as it put them upon the watch, and they guarded themselves against the evil accordingly.

He that longeth after the interpretation of the deeds of Henry, let him go and make inquiry of those who acted with him, the ministers of the *Hartford Convention*.

Now, there was a certain hypocrite whose name was *Elijah*, and he was a false prophet in the east, and led astray those of little understanding: moreover, he was an hireling, and preached for the sake of filthy lucre.

And he rose up and called himself a preacher of the gospel, and his words were smooth, and the people marvelled at him;

But he profaned the temple of the Lord, and he strove to lead his disciples into the wrong way.

And many wise men turned their backs against him; nevertheless he repented not of his sins unto this day.

Neither did the people, as Darius the Mede did unto the prophet Daniel, cast him into the den of lions, that they might see whether the royal beasts would disdain to devour him.

But they were rejoiced that power was down from heaven to consume the friends of the great Sanhedrim.

CHAP. V.

American Army—Militia—Navy—-British Navy—Rogers' First Cruise—capture Of the U. S. Brig Nautilus—removal of aliens beyond tide-water.

The whole host of the people of Columbia, who had been trained to war, being numbered, was about seven thousand fighting men.[5]

Neither were they assembled together; but they were extended from the north to the south, about three thousand miles.[6]

But the husbandmen, who lived under their own fig-trees, and lifted the arm in defence of their own homes, were more than seven hundred thousand, all mighty men of valor.

Now the armies of the king of Britain, are they not numbered and written in the book of *Hume*, the scribe? is not their name a terror to all nations?

Moreover, the number of the strong ships of the peaceable inhabitants of Columbia, that moved on the waters of the deep, carrying therein the destroying engines, which vomited their thunders, was about one score; besides a handful of "cock-boats;" with "a bit of striped bunting at their masthead."

But the number of the fighting vessels of Britain was about one thousand one score and one, which bore the royal cross.

---

[5] Standing army.
[6] From District of Maine to Mobile bay and New-Orleans.

And the men of war of Britain were arrayed in their might against the people of the land of Columbia.

Nevertheless, it came to pass, that about this time a strong ship of the United States, called the *President*, commanded by a skillful man whose name was *Rogers*,[7]

Sailed towards the island of Britain, and went nigh unto it, and made captive numbers of the vessels of the people of Britain, in their own waters; after which she returned in safety to the land of Columbia.

And the people gave much praise to Rogers, for it was a cunning thing; inasmuch as he saved many ships that were richly laden, so that they fell not into the hands of the people of Britain.

Moreover, it happened about the fifteenth day of the seventh month, in the same year in which the decree of the great Sanhedrim was issued, that a certain vessel of the states of Columbia was environed round about by a multitude of the ships of the king;

And the captain thereof was straitened, and he looked around him, and strove to escape:

But he was entrapped, and fell a prey to the vessels the king; howbeit, the captain, whose name was *Crane*, tarnished not his honor thereby.

And the name of the vessel of the United States was called *Nautilus*.

Now, about this time, there was a law sent forth from the great Sanhedrim, commanding all servants and subjects of the king of Britain forthwith to depart beyond the swellings of the waters of the great deep; even two score miles.

---

[7] Com. Rogers.

And they did so; and their friends from whom they were compelled to flee, mourned for them many days.

After this they could do no evil, on the which their hearts were bent continually.

And when they arrived in the back parts of the far extended provinces of Columbia, the husbandmen opened their mouths, and the dumb beasts looked at them with astonishment.

Neither doth the scribe marvel at their astonishment; for were not the servants of the king astonished, out of measure, at the brave men, of Columbia.

CHAP. VI.

Hull's expedition—he enters Canada, and encamps at Sandwich—issues his Proclamation—retreats to Detroit.

Now it was known throughout the land of Columbia that war was declared against the kingdom of Britain.

And to a certain chief captain called *William*, whose sur-name was *Hull*, was given in trust a band of more than two thousand chosen men, to go forth to battle in the north.[8]

Now Hull was a man well stricken in years, and he had been a captain in the host of Columbia, in the days that tried men's souls; even in the days of WASHINGTON.

Therefore, when he appeared in the presence of the great Sanhedrim,[9] they were pleased with his countenance, and put much faith in him.

Moreover, he was a governor in the north,[10] and a man of great wealth.

And, now when he arrived with his army hard by the *Miami of the Lakes*, he got him a vessel and placed therein those things which were appertaining unto the preservation of the lives of the sick and the maimed.

But, in an evil hour, the vessel was ensnared, near unto a strong hold,[11] beside a river, called in the language of the Gauls, *Detroit*.

---

[8] Canada

[9] Gen. Hull had been to Washington and obtained an appointment previous to the war.

[10] Michigan territory.

[11] Malden

And the army of the provinces of Columbia suffered much thereby.

Nevertheless, on the twelfth of the seventh month, about the fourth watch of the night, William with his whole host crossed the river which is called Detroit.

And he encamped his men round about the town of *Sandwich* in the province of the king.

From this place, he sent forth a Proclamation, which the great Sanhedrim had prepared for him; and the wisdom thereof appeareth even unto this day.

But if a man's ass falleth into a ditch, shall the master suffer thereby? if injury can be prevented, shall we not rather with our might endeavor to help him?

Now in the proclamation which Hull published abroad, he invited the people of the province of Canada to join themselves to the host of Columbia, who were come to drive the servants of the king from their borders.

And it came to pass, that a great multitude flocked to the banners of the great Sanhedrim.

Nevertheless, they knew not that they were to be entrapt.

However it was so, that William departed from the province of the king, and again passed the river.

And when the husbandmen of the province of Canada, who had joined the standard of Columbia, learned those things, they wept bitterly; for they were left behind.

After this William secured himself in the strong hold of Detroit; and the eyes of the men and the WOMEN of Columbia were fixed upon him.

And the expectation thereof may be likened unto a man who hath watered well his vineyard.

CHAP. VII.

Hull's expedition—surrender of his army and the whole Michigan territory—his trial and pardon by the President—capture of Michilimackinack.

Now the host of the king were few in numbers; nevertheless, they came in battle array against the strong hold of William.

And when he beheld them from afar, he was afraid; his knees smote one against another, and his heart sunk within him; for, lo! the savages of the wilderness appeared amongst them.

And a rumor went throughout the camp of Columbia, and it bore hard upon William.

Inasmuch as they said the wickedness of his heart was bent on giving up the strong hold to the servants of the king.

Howbeit he was not taxed with drinking of the strong waters of Jamaica; which when they enter into the head of a man, destroy his reason and make him appear like unto one who hath lost his senses.

And when the charge against William was made known unto the soldiers of Columbia, they were grieved much, for they were brave men, and feared nought.

So the officers communed one with another touching the thing: but they wist not what to do.[12]

---

[12] The officers present were not sufficiently numerous to warrant any opposition to the weakness of the general.

And they fain would have done violence unto William, that they might have been enabled to pour forth their thunders against the approaching host of Britain; which he had forbidden to be done.

Moreover, the names of these valiant men, who were compelled to weep before the cowardice of William, are they not recorded in the bosom of every friend of Columbian liberty?[13]

And it was about the sixteenth of the eighth month when the servants of the king appeared before the strong hold of Detroit.

And the name of the chief captain of the province of Canada, that came against the strong hold, was Brock, whose whole force was about seven hundred soldiers of the king, and as many savages.

Now when the soldiers of Canada were distant about a furlong, moving towards the strong hold; even when the destroying engines were ready to utter their thunders, and smite them to the earth,

William, whose heart failed him, commanded the valiant men of Columbia to bow down before the servants of the king;

And he ordered them to yield up the destructive weapons which they held in their hands.

Neither could they appear in battle against the king again in many days.

Moreover, the cowardice of his heart caused him to make a league with the slaves of the king, in the which he gave unto them the whole territory over which the people had entrusted him to preside; notwithstanding it appertained not unto him.

---

[13] Miller, Cass, McArthur, Brush, Findley, &c.

And the balls of solid iron, and the black dust, and the destroying engines became a prey unto the men of Britain.

Now there had followed after William a band of brave men from the west,(13) and the name of their captain was *Brush*; and he had in trust the bread and the wine which were to support the army of Columbia.

And, lest they should fall into the hands of the savages, a captain, whose name was Vanhorn, was ordered to go forth and meet him.

And the band that went forth, was entrapped at Brownstown, by the cunning savages, that laid wait for them, and the killed and the wounded of Columbia were about two score.

And again there were sent from the camp of William more than five hundred men to go to the aid of Brush.

And the name of the chief captain thereof, was *Miller*[14] and the captain whom he ordered to go before him was called *Snelling*.[15]

Now Snelling was a valiant man, and strove hard against the men of Britain, and the savages; even until Miller the chief captain arrived.

And the place, which is called *Maguago*, lieth about an hundred furlongs distant from Detroit.

Now the battle waxed hot; and the host of Miller pressed hard upon the savages and upon the men of Britain.
Inasmuch as they were compelled to flee before the arms of Columbia: and Miller gat great honor thereby.

And there fell of the men of Britain that day an hundred two score and ten.

---

[14] Col. Miller,
[15] Col. J. Snelling.

Nevertheless, in the league which William had made, he had included Miller, and all the brave captains and men of war of Columbia that were nigh the place.

Now, therefore, whether it was cowardice outright, in William, or whether he became treacherous for filthy lucre's sake, appeareth not unto the scribe.[16]

But the effect thereof to the nation, was as a man having a millstone cast about his neck.

So William and his whole army fell into the hands of the servants of the king.

But as it is written in the book of Solomon, There is a time for all things, so it came to pass, afterwards, that William was called to account for his evil deeds.

And he was examined before the lawful tribunal of his country, and they were all valiant warriors and chief captains in the land of Columbia.

Howbeit, when the council[17] had weighed well the matter, they declared him *guilty*, and ordered that he should suffer death.

Nevertheless, they recommended him to the mercy of James, the chief governor of the land of Columbia.

Saying, Lo! the wickedness of the man appeareth unto us as the noon day;

---

[16] To palliate Hull's conduct it has been urged, that he surrendered his army to prevent the effusion of blood: but let us ask those charitable palliators what they would have said of Gen. Jackson, if, when a mighty and a blood-thirsty enemy appeared before his battlements, in quest of beauty and booty, he had given up N. Orleans and ceded the Louisiana territory to him? or of the gallant Croghan, when left to defend fort Stephenson with a handful of men and a single six pounder ?—These *palliators* might even have *wished* that the heroes of Erie and Champlain had felt the same qualms of conscience:—but they ought to know that it was such noble deeds that stopt the *"effusion blood."*

[17] Court-martial.

But the infirmities of his age have weakened his understanding, therefore let his gray hairs go down into the grave in silence.

And when James heard the words of the council, his heart melted as wax before the fire.

And he said, Lo! ye have done that which seemeth right unto me.

Nevertheless, as my soul hopeth for mercy, for this thing William shall not surely die; but his name shall be blotted out from the list of the brave.

For it appeareth unto me that he was possessed of an evil spirit, and wist not what he did.

Notwithstanding this, William thanked him not, but added insult to cowardice.[18]

So William was ordered to depart to the land which lieth in the east,[19] where he remaineth unto this day; and his name shall be no more spoken of with reverence amongst men.

Moreover, there was another evil which fell upon the people of the United States, about the time the host of Columbia crossed the river Detroit.

For, lo! the strong hold of *Michilimackinack*, which lieth nigh unto the Lakes of *Michigan* and *Huron* fell an easy prey unto the men of Britain, and their red brethren;

Howbeit, their numbers were more than four-fold greater than the men of Columbia, who knew not of the war.

---

[18] Hull's address to the public.
[19] Massachusetts,

Nevertheless, the people of the United States, even the great Sanhedrim, were not disheartened; neither were they afraid; for they had counted the cost, and were prepared to meet the evil.

CHAP. VIII.

Capture of the British frigate Guerriere, by the united states' frigate constitution, captain hull—capture of the Alert Sloop of war, by the Essex, Captain Porter.

Now it came to pass, on the nineteenth day of the eighth month, that one of the tall ships of Columbia, called the *Constitution*, commanded by *Isaac* whose sur-name was *Hull*,

Having spread her snowy wings on the bosom of the mighty deep, beheld from afar one of the fighting ships of Britain bearing the royal cross.

And the name of the ship was called, in the language of the French, *Guerriere*,[20] which signifieth a warrior, and *Dacres* was the captain thereof.

Now when Dacres beheld the ship of Columbia his eyes sparkled with joy, for he had defied the vessels of Columbia.

And he spake unto his officers and his men that were under him, saying,

Let every man be at his post, and ere the glass hath passed the third part of an hour, her stripes shall cease to sweep the air of heaven.

And the yawning deep shall open its mouth to receive the enemies of the king.

---

[20] The Guerriere was taken from the French by the British.

And the men of Dacres shouted aloud, and drank of the strong waters of Jamaica, which make men mad; moreover they mixed the black dust therewith.

Now when Isaac drew nigh unto the king's ship the people of Columbia shouted.

And Isaac bore down upon the strong ship of the king.

About this time they put the lighted match to the black dust of the destroying engines, and it was like unto a clap of thunder.

Moreover, the fire and smoke issued out of the mouths of the engines in abundance, so as to darken the air, and they were overshadowed by the means thereof.

(Now the black dust was not known among the ancients; even Solomon, in all his wisdom, knew it not.)

And the battle continued with tremendous roar until about the space of half an hour, when its noises ceased.

But when the clouds of smoke had passed away, behold! the mighty GUERRIERE lay a sinking wreck upon the face of the waters.

The shadow of hope passed over her as a dream; and most reluctantly was she compelled to strike the lion's red cross to the eagle of Columbia.

Whilst the CONSTITUTION, like *Shadrach* in the fiery furnace, filled her white sails and passed along as though nothing had happened unto her.

Now the slain and the maimed of the king that day were five score and five.

And the loss of the people of Columbia, was seven slain and seven wounded.

After this Isaac caused a burning coal to be placed in the ship that she might be consumed, and the flames thereof mounted towards the heavens.

And the great Sanhedrim honored Isaac with great honor, and the people were rejoiced in him, and they forgat the evils which had befallen them in the north.

But when the lords and counsellors of Britain heard those things they believed them not; it was as the bitterness of gall to their souls; for the pride of Britain was fixed upon her navy; it was the apple of her eye.

Now, as one evil followeth after another to the sons of men, so it happened that, in the same month, a certain strong ship of the United States, even the *Essex*, the name of the captain whereof, was *Porter*, sailed in search of the vessels of the king, on the waters of the ocean.

And in process of time, she fell upon one of the ships of Britain, called the *Alert*, and made spoil thereof to the people of Columbia.

CHAP. IX.

Attack on Sackett's Harbor—affair of Ogdensburgh—British drove from St. Regis, by the Troy militia under major young— the brigs Adams and Caledonia re-captured by Capt. Elliot, near fort Erie.

Now the movements of the enemy were as the motion of a whirlwind, which passeth from the north to the south, and from the east to the west.

And they sought to encompass the whole land of Columbia round about.

So it came to pass that a number of the armed vessels of the king, that sailed on the great lake which is called *Ontario*, moved toward *Sackett's Harbor*.

And they demanded certain vessels of the people of the United States, which they had taken from the king, to be given up unto them, saying:

Verily, if ye give them not up, then will we lay a contribution upon you, and ye shall pay tribute.

But *Bellinger*, the chief captain of the Harbor, refused.

And when the vessels of the king were hard by, a certain captain whose name was *Woolsey*, set one of the engines to work.

And the vessels of the king also opened the mouths of their engines and shot into the camp of Columbia.

And the number of the husbandmen of the United States that flocked to the defence of the Harbor was about three thousand.

And when the men of war of Britain saw that the people of Columbia were not afraid, and that they knew to use the destroying engines, they fled to their strong hold, in the province of the king, which is called *Kingston*.

Howbeit, some of their ships received much damage from the balls of heavy metal, that smote them, from the strong hold.

Now as the malice of the nations increased one against another, so did the evils increase which surrounded them.

And it came to pass on the fourth day of the tenth month, there came a thousand fighting men of Britain to lay waste the village of *Ogdensburg*, which lieth hard by the river *St. Lawrence*.

Howbeit, the people of Columbia permitted them not to come unto the land; but compelled them to depart in haste.

Nigh unto this place is a village Which is called *St. Regis*, where the soldiers of Britain had come to fix a strong hold, on the borders of Columbia.

But a brave captain, Whose name was Young, with a band of men, called militia, went against them.

And he sat the destroying engines to work, and the noise thereof sounded in their ears; so they were discomfitted and fled in confusion.

And the number of the servants of the king, made captive that day, was two score men, with the instruments of destruction in their hands.

Moreover, one of the banners of the king, even the red-cross standard of Britain, fell into the hands of Young.

On the eighth day of the same month, a captain, of Columbia, whose name was *Elliot*, a Gunning man, took a chosen band, who came from the sea-coast, and put them in boats.

And he departed with them from *Niagara* towards the strong hold of *Erie*, even in the dead of the night.

And he came unawares upon the two vessels which were covenanted to the king, with the army at Detroit.

And the name of the vessels were the *Adams* and the *Caledonia*, and Elliot captured them the same night.

However, the next day, as Elliot and his men were returning with their prizes, the men of Britain, who were upon the other shore, let the destroying engines loose upon them from their strong hold;

And a few of the people of Columbia were slain; moreover, it was here the valiant *Cuyler* fell; a ball of heavy metal struck him as he was coming on a fleet horse toward the water's edge.

Now Cuyler was a man well beloved; and the officers and men of Columbia grieved for him many days.

CHAP. X.

Battle of Queenstown—the British General Brock killed.

And it came to pass on the morning of the thirteenth day of the tenth month,

That Stephen, a chief captain of Columbia, sur-named *Van Rensselaer,* essayed to cross the river which is called *Niagara,* with his whole army.

Now the river lieth between the Lake *Erie* and the Lake *Ontario,*

And the noise of the waters of the river is louder than the roarings of the forest; yea, it is like unto the rushing of mighty armies to battle.

And the movement of the falls thereof bringeth the people from all parts of the earth to behold it.[21]

So Stephen gat his soldiers into the boats that were prepared for them, and they moved upon the rough waters of the river, toward the strong hold of *Queenstown.*

And when the men of Britain saw them approach, they opened the engines upon them, from *Fort George, Erie,* and *Black Rock.*

Nevertheless, they persevered; although the strength of the waters, which were ungovernable, separated the army.

However, *Solomon,*[22] a captain and a kinsman of Stephen, reached the shore with the men under his command, in all about two hundred.

---

[21] Niagara falls.
[22] Col. Solomon Van Rensselaer.

And he put the army in battle array, in a valley, and moved up towards the strong hold; and *Brock* was the chief captain of the host of Britain.

And from their strong hold they shot, with their mischievous engines, balls of lead in abundance; and it was as a shower of hail upon the people of Columbia;

For there was no turning to the right hand nor to the left for safety.

And Solomon and his men fought hard; and they rushed into the hottest of the battle.

And Solomon and his men fought hard; and they rushed into the hottest of the battle.

And a captain of the United States, whose name was Chrystie, followed close after them, with a chosen band of brave men.

So they pushed forward to the strong hold, and drove the men of Britain before them, like sheep, and smote them hip and thigh, with great slaughter; and Brock, their chief captain, was among the slain.

And Chrystie, and the valiant *Wool*, and *Ogilvie*, and the host of Columbia gat into the hold, and the army of the king fled: and *Chrystie* was wounded in the palm of his band.

But Solomon was sorely wounded, so that his strength tailed him, and he went not into the hold.

And that day there fell of the servants of the king many valiant men, even those who were called invincibles, and bad gained great honor in Egypt.

Nevertheless, the same day a mighty host of savages and soldiers of the king,[23] came forth again to battle, and rushed upon the people of the United States, and drove them from the strong hold of Queenstown.

For, lo! Stephen, the chief captain, could not prevail on the host of militia, on the other side of the river, to cross over.

So the army of Columbia moved down towards the river to cross over again, that they might escape.

But when they came down to the water side, lo! they were deceived, for there was not a boat to convey them to a place of safety; so they became captives to the men of Britain.

Now the men of Britain treated the prisoners kindly, and showed much tenderness towards them; for which the people blessed them.

And the killed and wounded of the host of Columbia, were an hundred two score and ten.

And the prisoners that fell into the hands of the king, were about seven hundred.

Nevertheless, in a letter which Stephen sent to Henry[24] the chief captain of the army of the north, he gave great honor unto the captains who fought under him that day.

And the names of the valiant men, who distinguished themselves in the battle, were *Wadsworth, Van Rensselaer, Scott, Chrystie, Fenwick, Fink, Gibson*, and many other brave men of war.

---

[23] Reinforcements from Fort George and Chippawa.
[24] Maj. Gen. Dearborn.

CHAP. XI.

Gen. Smyth Succeeds Gen. Van Rensselaer— his Attempt to Cross the Niagara, And Failure —causes.

After these things, on the same day in which the letter was written, Stephen resigned the command of his army to a certain chief captain whose name was *Alexander*.[25]

Now Alexander was a man well skilled in the arts of warfare.

And he made a proclamation to the young men of the state of New-York, wherein he invited them to go forth from their homes, and join the host under him.

And the words thereof pleased the young men, so that they went in numbers and joined Alexander; on the shores of the river which is called the Niagara.

But here the hand of the scribe trembleth, his tongue faltereth, his heart sickeneth, and be would fain blot from his memory that which truth compels him to record; for he is a living witness thereof.

Alas, there was an evil spirit moving in secret, and in bye-places throughout the land of Columbia; and it was the offspring of tyranny, the cup-bearer of royalty; Toryism.

And lo! its viper-like insidiousness crept into the ears of the unwary husbandmen.

---

[25] Brig. Gen. Smyth.

For the sect of the tories whispered unto them, saying, Lo! the laws of the land cannot compel you to step over the borders of the United States.

Moreover, said they, the fierceness the savages is terrible as the wild tyger, and their numbers as the trees of the forest.

And the veteran soldiers of the king, who have been bred to war, are spread in multitudes over the province of Canada.

Therefore, if ye go over to fight against them, ye will be as sheep going to the slaughter, and ye shall never again return to the house of your fathers, for ye will be destroyed.

Even as the wickedness of the war, which the great Sanhedrim have made, against the king, cannot prosper, so shall ye fall a prey to the folly thereof.

And it came to pass when the husbandmen heard these smooth words, many of them were bewildered in their minds, and knew not what to do.

So when the young men who had flocked to the banners of Alexander, came down to the water's edge, to go into the boats, they thought of the words which the enemies of Columbia had spoken unto them; and they refused to cross over:

Neither could the persuasions of the chief captain prevail on them all to go into the boats; and those whose hearts were willing were not enough.

So he was obliged to suffer them to return to their homes; for his expectations were blasted.

And the army of Columbia went into winter quarters; for the earth was covered with snow, and the waters of the great lakes were congealed.

CHAP. XII.

Capture of the sloop of war Frolic, of 22 guns, by the United States' sloop of war wasp, of 18 guns.

Now the strong ships of war of the kingdom of Britain were spread over the whole face of the waters of the ocean.

But few, indeed, were the vessels of Columbia, that were fighting ships and carried the destroying engines.

Howsoever, early in the morning of the eighteenth day of the tenth month, about the sixth hour, being on the sabbath day,

One of the ships of Columbia, called the *Wasp*, the name of the captain whereof was *Jones*, who was a valiant man, discovered afar off one of the strong ships of the king.

Now the ship of Britain was mightier than the ship of Columbia, and she was called the *Frolic*, and the captain's name was *Whinycates*.

And they began to utter their thunders about the eleventh hour of the day, and the noises continued for more than the space of half an hour.

When the Wasp, falling upon the Frolic, and getting entangled therewith, the men struggled together; and the mariners of Columbia overpowered the mariners of Britain.

So it came to pass, that the Frolic became captive to the ship of Columbia.

And the slain and the wounded of the king's ship were about four score.

And the children of Columbia lost, in all, about half a score: howbeit, there was much damage done to both vessels.

Nevertheless, about this time, a mighty ship of Britain, called the *Poictiers*, came upon the vessels, which were in a defenceless situation, and took them both, and commanded them to go to the island of the king

However, the people of Columbia were pleased with the noble conduct of Jones, and for his valiant acts they gave him a sword of curious workmanship.

Moreover, while he remained at Bermuda, the inhabitants, the servants of the king, treated him kindly; and showed much respect for him and his officers that were made captive.

CHAP. XIII.

Capture of the British frigate Macedonian, by Com. Decatur, in the frigate United States —brig vixen captured by the British frigate Southampton.

Now it happened on the twenty-fifth day of the tenth month, in the first year of the war, that a certain strong ship of Britain, that had prepared herself to fight a ship of Columbia, appeared upon the waters of the deep.

And she was commanded by a valiant captain whose name was *Carden*, and the name of the ship was the *Macedonian*.

And on the same day she met one of the strong ships of Columbia, the name of the captain whereof was *Decatur*, and the vessel was called the *United States*.

Now Decatur was a man who had never known fear; and the good of his country was the pride of his heart.

And when he came towards the vessel of the king, he used no entreaty with his men, for they all loved him, and the point of his finger was as the word of his mouth.

So when the ships came nigh unto one another, their thunders were tremendous, and the smoke thereof was as a black cloud.

Nevertheless, in the space of about ninety minutes, the strong ship of Britain struck her red flag to the simple stripes of Columbia.

Now the Macedonian was a new ship, and she gat much damage.

But the United States, like the companions of Shadrach, moved unhurt upon the waters; nay, even her wings were not singed.

And the slain and the wounded, of the ship of the king, were five score and four.

And there fell of the people of Columbia five who were slain outright, and there were seven maimed.

Moreover the ship of Britain had seven of the stolen men of Columbia therein, who were compelled to fight against their brethren; and two of them were slain in battle.

And when Carden came on board the ship of Columbia, he bowed his head, and offered to put his sword, of curious workmanship, into the hands of Decatur.

But Decatur said unto him, Nay; thou hast defended thy ship like a valiant man; therefore, keep thy sword, but receive my hand.

So they sat down and drank wine together, for the spirits of brave men mingle even in the time of warfare.

And after they had eaten and drank, Carden opened his mouth, for he was troubled in his mind, and spake unto Decatur, saying:

Lo! if this thing which hath happened be known unto the king, that one of the vessels of Britain hath struck her flag, and become captive to a vessel of the United States, what shall be done unto the captain thereof? for such a thing hath not been heard of among the nations of the earth.

And Decatur answered, and spake unto Carden, saying, Verily thou art deceived, neither will harm happen unto thee.

For, lo! it came to pass, about three-score days ago, that one of the strong ships of the king, thy master, the name whereof was called Guerriere, fell an easy prey to one of the strong ships of Columbia; and they burnt her with fire upon the waters.

Now when Carden heard these words, his heart leaped with joy; for he dreaded the frowns of the king, and he was glad that he stood not alone in the thing.

After this, in the eighteen hundred and thirteenth year of the christian era, on the first day of the first month of the same year, and on the sixth day of the week,

The ship United States and the ship Macedonian came into the haven of New-York, having passed a certain dangerous place called *Hell-gate*: and there was a heavy fog that day.

And there were great rejoicings in the city, and throughout the whole land of Columbia.

Moreover, there was a sumptuous dinner given to Isaac, Decatur, and Jones, in honor of their valiant deeds; and the number of the guests were about five hundred.

And the inhabitants of New-York made a great feast, on the ninth day of the month, for the brave mariners that wrought in the ship of Columbia.

And they became merry with the drinking of wine; after which they departed and went unto a house of mirth and gaiety.[26]

Now, it is written in the words of Solomon, whose wisdom hath not been excelled, that, there is a time to weep, and a time to rejoice.

---

[26] Theatre.

Not many days after those things, it came to pass, that the hearts of the lords and the counsellors of Britain were rejoiced.

For a certain mighty ship, called the Southampton, fell upon a smaller vessel of the United States,[27] and made capture thereof unto the king.

But the storm arose, and the sea beat upon the vessels, and they were cast away, and they parted asunder, upon an island which lieth far to the south, and both vessels were lost.

---

[27] United States' brig Vixen, 12 guns, G. Reed commander.

CHAP. XIV.

Affairs in the north—skirmishes—battle of Frenchtown, on the river Raisin—capture of Gen. Winchester's army—massacre of American prisoners.

Now it came to pass, that the wickedness of Britain had roused up the spirit of Satan in the savages of the forest, in the north and in the west.

And the tomahawk and the scalping knife were raised against the people of Columbia on the borders of the great lakes.

So the people sought after a valiant man to go against the savages and the men of Britain.

And they pitched upon a certain governor of the west, whose name was *Harrison*,[28] and the great Sanhedrim made him a chief captain of the army.

Moreover, he was beloved by the people, and a mighty host of husbandmen were ready to follow after him.

And Harrison rested his army at the strong hold of *Meigs*, nigh the *Miami Rapids*, which lieth in the way journeying towards the strong hold of *Maiden*, which is in the province of the king; whither he intended to go forth in the pleasant season of the year.

And *Winchester*[29] was another chief captain that went against the savages.

---

[28] Maj. Gen. W. H. Harrison, Governor of Ohio.
[29] Brig. Gen. Winchester.

Now the savages had been a sore thorn in the side of the people of Columbia.

They had assailed the hold which is called after a chief captain whose name was *Dearborn*, and their numbers overpowered it, and they used deceit, and put to death the men and the women and the infants that were found in the hold, after they had become captives, save about half a score.

And their howlings along the dark forest were more terrible than the wild wolf, and their murderous cunning more dreadful than the prowling tiger.

And the servants of the king gave them to drink of the strong waters of Jamaica, well knowing that they loved it as they did their own souls.

Yet these were the allies, the messmates, the companions of the slaves of Britain! hired assassins!

However, about this time there were many brave captains of the people of the United States that went against them.

Even *Russel*, and *Hopkins*, and *Tupper*, and *Campbell*, and *Williams*, and others, who drove the red savages before them.

And burnt their villages,[30] and laid waste their habitations, and slew many of them; for it is written in the holy scripture, Blood for blood!

Nevertheless, they treated the savage prisoners who fell into their hands kindly; neither suffered they the people to buffet them.

But it came to pass, on the twenty-second day of the first month, a mighty horde of savages and servants of the king, fell upon the army of Winchester the chief captain.

---

[30] Towns on the Wabash.

And it was about the dawning of the day, when the destructive engines opened their fires.

And the place where the battle was fought was called, in the vernacular tongue, *Frenchtown*, which lieth on the south side of the *River Raisin*, nigh unto Lake Erie.

Now the name of the chief captain of the army of Britain was *Proctor*, and he proved himself a wicked man, and his name is despised even unto this day.

Howsoever, the battle waxed hot, and they began to rush one upon another with great violence.

And the small band of Columbia fought desperately, and the slaughter was dreadful; and the pure snow of heaven was sprinkled and stained with the blood of men!

Nevertheless, the people of the United States were overcome, and their chief captain made prisoner.

So when Winchester found he was made captive, and that there was no hope for the rest of the men under his command, he made a league with Proctor, the chief captain of the host of the king.

In the which Proctor agreed to vouch-safe protection to the captive men of Columbia, from the wrath of the savages, whom he had inflamed.

Now the number of the men of Columbia that fell into their hands that day, were about five hundred; and the slain and wounded about an hundred two score and ten.

And the number of the savages and the men of Britain who fell in battle that day were many.

And Proctor removed the captives unto the strong hold of Malden, which lieth upon the opposite side of the river, in the province of the king.

But, in the cruelty of his heart, he left the sick, the wounded, and the dying to the mercy of the savages of the wilderness!

In this thing he transgressed the word of a man, which is evil in the sight of the Lord.

Oh! for a veil, to hide in utter darkness the horrid deeds of that awful day, that they might not be handed down to the children of men, in the times to come.

Lo! early in the morning of the next day, ere the sun had risen, the work of death began!

Behold the sullen savage, with deadly rage, drag forth the shivering soldier over the blood-stained snow, fainting, bleeding with his wounds, and imploring on his knees for mercy.

Alas! the savage understandeth not his words; but giveth him a blow with the hatchet of death.

For have not the counsellors of Britain said, For this will we give unto you silver and gold?

Thus were the poor wounded prisoners of Columbia slaughtered in abundance.

And *Round-Head*, the chief captain of the warriors, and the savages under him, gat great praise from Proctor, the chief captain of the host of Britain.[31]

Neither did the sick and wounded escape, who had gathered themselves together in the houses, that they might be sheltered from the piercing cold; even those who were weary and unable to go forth.

---

[31] See Proctor's account of the battle, dated Quebec, February 8, 1813.

For the savages put the burning brand to the houses, from which they could not flee, and burnt them alive therein.

And the flames and the smoke arose! and their cries and their groans reached the high chancery of heaven,

Where they will stand recorded, until the coming of that Day for which all other days were made.

Lo! are those the helpmates of the mighty kingdom of Britain? that noble and generous nation, the bulwark of religion?

Tell it not in Gath; publish it not in the streets of Askalon.[32]

---

[32] The whole of this massacre was conducted under the eyes of the British officers, and sanctioned by them as well as by their government; for this fact has never been disavowed.

CHAP. XV.

Capture of the British Frigate java, by the United States frigate Constitution.

In the twelfth month of the first year of the decree of the great Sanhedrim, on the twenty and ninth day of the month,

It came to pass, that one of the strong ships of the king had approached the country of the south, which lieth many thousand miles off.

And the ship was called *Java*, after one of the sweet scented islands of the east; where the poppy flourishes, where the heat of the sun is abundant, and where the Bohon Upas emits its deadly poison.

Moreover, she carried about four hundred and fifty men, and a governor,[33] and many officers and soldiers of the king; and she was well prepared for battle.

And Lambert commanded the ship of Britain, and he was a brave and valiant man.

So as be passed along, nigh unto the coast of Brazil, where the sun casteth the shadow of a man to the south at noon day:

(A place unknown to the children of Israel, in the days of Moses)

---

[33] Gov. Hyslop and suite, bound to Bombay, in the East Indies.

Lo! one of the tall ships of Columbia, even the Constitution, beheld her when she was yet a great way off, and made signs unto her which she answered not.

Which caused the gallant captain, whose sur-name was Bainbridge,[34] to cast a shot towards her, after which she received the thunder of his destroying engines.

And it was about the second hour after the mid-day, when the sound of the battle-drum was heard.

And as they approached towards each other the people shouted aloud, and the roaring of the engines was dreadful.

And the servants of the king fought bravely; and they held out to the last.

For they were ashamed to let the nations of the earth say unto them,

Lo! ye, who are the lords and the masters of the mighty deep, have suffered these feeble[35] Yankees to conquer you.

Therefore, the slaughter was dreadful, beyond measure.

And the black clouds of smoke arose, and obscured the rays of the sun, so that they fought in the shade thereof.

And the winds moved the vessels about, and they strove to avoid the balls of lead, and the heavy balls of iron, that whistled about them in multitudes.

(Now these balls, which were gathered from the bowels of the earth, were unknown to the Philistines; even Sampson was a stranger to them.)

---

[34] Com. Bainbridge.
[35] Anacreon Moore, by this time, it is hoped, is sufficiently convinced of the effeminacy of the Americans.

However, the ships fought hard, for the space of about two hours, when their thunders ceased.

And the ship of Britain had become a wreck, and the deck thereof was covered with blood!

Nevertheless, the servants of the king struck not the flag of Britain; for they were loth, and hesitated:

But when Bainbridge, who saw this, came down upon them a second time, they humbled themselves, and drew down the British cross.

And the slain and the wounded of the king, that day, were an hundred three score and ten;

And those of the people of Columbia, were about thirty and four.

Moreover, Bainbridge, the captain of the vessel of the United States, was sorely wounded.

And Lambert, the captain of the ship of the king was wounded, even unto death.

Now, after the servants of the king were taken from the wreck, and meat and drink sat before them, that they might be refreshed, they regaled themselves, and were thankful.

And on the second day Bainbridge put a match to the black dust that remained in the ship, and she burst asunder, and rent the air with a loud noise.

And the fragments thereof were spread upon the waters round about.

And the fish of the sea, even the mighty whales, fled from the noise of the ship.

However, the Constitution escaped not unhurt, for she was much wounded in her tackling.

So, when Bainbridge came into the haven of *St. Salvador*, which lieth farther to the south, he gave the men of Britain, whom he had made captive, liberty to go home to the king, their master.

But when the tidings thereof reached the palace of the king, the lords and the princes and the rulers of Britain were confounded.

Their spirits sunk within them: astonishment seized the tyrants of the ocean.

The smile of joy had departed from their countenances, and the gloom of despair hovered around them.

The wise men and the orators were mute; they gaped one upon another, and wist not what to say.

But the people of Columbia, from the north to the south, were gladdened; and bestowed great honor and praise on Bainbridge the captain.

Even the great Sanhedrim of the people rejoiced with great joy.

CHAP. XVI.

Com. Rogers' return from a second cruise— capture of the United States' brig Viper—the general Armstrong and a British frigate—privateering.

Now it came to pass, in the beginning of the one thousand eight hundred and thirteenth year of the Great Founder of the Christian sect,

That a strong ship of the United States, called the *President,* commanded by *Rogers,* returned a second time to the land of Columbia.

And while she was upon the waters of the great deep, she fell in with one of the packets of the king, called after the swift-flying bird[36] of the air, and made capture thereof.

And in the ship Rogers found abundance of wealth; even an hundred, sixty and eight thousand pieces of silver.

And it was carried, with many horses, to a place of safe-keeping,[37] in the town of *Boston,* which lieth to the east.

Moreover, he made capture of another ship of the king,[38] laden with oil and bones of the great fish of the deep.

Now it happened, on the seventeenth day of the first month of the same year,

---

[36] Swallow.
[37] State Bank of Boston.
[38] United States' brig Viper.

That one of the weak vessels of the United States,[39] became a prey to one of the strong ships of the king, called the *Narcissus*; albeit she fought not.

About this time the great waters of the Chesapeake, which empty into the sea, were guarded by the strong ships of the king, so that the vessels might not arrive or depart therefrom.

But the vessels of the United States, and the private vessels of the men of Columbia, were doing great damage unto the commerce of Britain, even in her own waters.

And the number of the private vessels, that moved swiftly over the face of the waters, and went out to despoil the commerce of Britain, and make capture merchant vessels thereof, was about two hundred, two score and ten.

And they made capture of more than fifteen hundred of the vessels of the people of Britain.[40]

Moreover, there was a sore battle between one of the private armed vessels of the people of the United States, and a strong ship of the king.[41]

The privateer was called the *General Armstrong*, and the name of the captain was *Guy*.[42]

Now Guy was a valiant man, and fear was a stranger to him.

And on the eleventh day of the third month, he espied from afar a vessel which appeared as a speck upon the waters.

But when he bore down upon her, behold! she was a fighting ship of Britain, carrying the destroying engines.

---

[39] Ship Argo.
[40] During the war.
[41] A British frigate.
[42] Capt. Champlin.

And Guy was nigh being entrapped, for he was deceived, thinking it a merchant's ship.

Therefore he was compelled to fight, so he opened upon the vessel of the king one of his mischievous engines called, in the vernacular tongue, *long-tom*.

And they fought hard, and the noise of the engines was very great.

And the balls of lead and iron showered around like hail-stones; for the strong ship of Britain had them in abundance.

Now the slaughter was dreadful on both sides, and Guy was nigh making capture of the ship: but he received a wound and his vessel was disabled, so he made good his escape.

And the slain and the wounded of Guy were twenty and three, and the vessel of the king lost about twice that number.

Now, for this valiant act, Guy gat great honor, and the people gave him a sword of curious workmanship.

Moreover, the *Saratoga*, the *Scourge*, the *Chasseur*, and many other private vessels of the people of the United States, were a grievous plague to the servants of the king;

Inasmuch as some of them made sport with the mighty blockade of Britain, which she put forth against the free people of the land of Columbia.

For when they came nigh unto the coast of Britain, they made capture and burnt the vessels of the king, that carried rich merchandise, costly jewels, and silver and gold.

Yea, even in their own waters, and in the sight of their own havens, did they do these things.

For it happened that the cunning Yankees knew how to construct the swift-sailing vessels, that they out-ran the strong vessels of Britain.

And as the ships of Britain moved but slowly on the waters, so they caught them not.

Wherefore the artificers, the mechanics, and those who dealt in merchandise, raised their voices to the great council of Britain, saying,

Lo! are we not the faithful servants of the king, our master? have we not given unto him the one half of our whole substance? and shall these Yankees take from us the remainder?

Hath not the king a thousand ships of war? and wherefore should we be hemmed in?

Lo! our merchant vessels are idle! neither can we pass in safety even unto the land of Hibernia, which lieth nigh unto us.

And, behold, the captain of a private armed vessel of the Yankees, in derision of the proclamation of our lord the king, hath proclaimed the island of Great Britain and her dependencies in a state of rigorous blockade; saying, Lo! I have the power to hem ye in;

Therefore, let the counsellors of the king ponder these things, and let the strong ships of Britain drive the vessels of Columbia from our coast.

Now the wise men of Britain heard those things with sorrow; and they spake one to another concerning the matter:

But they wist not what to do; for the cunning of the captains of the fast sailing vessels of Columbia, surpassed the wisdom of the lords of Britain.

CHAP. XVII.

Capture and burning of Ogdensburgh by the British.

In these days the war against Columbia was waged with great violence.

And the fur- clad savages prowled in secret places and fell upon the helpless.

'They hid themselves in the wilderness; they couched down as a lion; and as a young lion, they watched for their prey.'

The tall and leafless trees of the forest bent to the strong winds of the north; and the sound thereof was as the roaring of mighty waters.

Moreover, the face of the earth was covered with snow, and the water of the rivers was frozen.

And the borders of Columbia, nigh unto the province of the king, were exposed to the transgressions of the enemy.

And the soldiers of the king came in abundance from the island of Britain, and pitched their tents in the Canadian provinces.

Accordingly, it came to pass, on the twenty-second day of the second month, being the birth-day of WASHINGTON, the deliverer,

That a mighty host came out of the province of the king, and went against the town of *Ogdensburgh,* and made capture thereof.

And there were five slain and ten wounded of the people of Columbia, and about three score were taken by the servants of the king.

Moreover, the men of Britain gat much spoil; even a multitude of the black dust fell into their hands;

And twelve of the destroying engines, which the people of Columbia had taken from the king, about forty years before.

Also, three hundred tents, and more than a thousand weapons of war; but the vessels and the boats, they consumed with fire.

Now Ogdensburg was a beautiful village to behold; nevertheless they burned it with fire, and it became a heap of ruins.

And the women and the children looked for their homes, but found them not; and they sat down in sorrow, for the haughty conquerors laughed at their sufferings.

After which they returned with their spoil to *Prescott*, from whence they came, being on the other side of the water, in the province of the king.

And the honor that was poured out upon the slaves of Britain that day was as a thimble full of water spilt into the sea: for they were like unto a giant going out against a bulrush.

CHAP. XVIII.

Capture of the Peacock, of 18 guns, by the U. S. Sloop of war hornet, of 16 guns—return of the Chesapeake from a cruise.

The deeds of the renowned warriors, the patriots, and the valiant men of Columbia, have prepared a path for the scribe, which he is compelled to follow.

But, as the soaring eagle moves to its craggy nest, or the cooing dove to its tender mate, so is the compulsion of his heart.

If the wickedness of Britain hath made manifest her folly; if her sons have sat down in sackcloth and ashes, the scribe looketh down upon her with pity.

It is written that, He who prideth himself in his strength shall be humbled; and the haughty shall be brought low.

And, if the Lord hath smiled upon the arms of Columbia, let no man frown.

Now it came to pass, in the eighteen hundred and thirteenth year of the Christian era, on the twenty-fourth day of the second month,

That one of the fighting vessels of Columbia, called the *Hornet*, which signifieth, in the vernacular tongue, a fly whose sting is poison,

Moved upon the great waters of the deep, far to the south, nigh unto a place which is called *Demarara*.

Moreover, the captain of the Hornet was a valiant man, and his name was *Lawrence*.

And it was towards the setting of the sun, when he came nigh unto one of the strong ships of the king, called the *Peacock*, after the bird whose feathers are beautiful to behold;

And the captain thereof was sur-named *Peake*.

Now began the roaring noises of the engines of destruction, that opened their mouths against one another; and dreadful was the slaughter of that day.

Nevertheless, in the space of about the fourth part of an hour the vessel of the king captured by the people of Columbia,

And they found therein some of the mariners of the United States, who had begged that they might go down into the hold of the ship, and not raise their hands against the blood of their own brethren:

But Peake, the commander, suffered them not, but compelled them to fight against their own kinsmen; and one of them was slain in battle.
And the killed and maimed of the people of Britain, were about two score and two; and Peake, the captain, was also slain: and the loss of Columbia was about five souls!

Moreover, the Peacock sunk down into the yawning deep, before they could get all the men of Britain out of her; and three of the people of Columbia were buried with her, whilst in the humane, act of endeavoring to preserve the lives of the enemy.

Now this was the fifth fighting vessel of the king which had been humbled, since the decree of the great Sanhedrim, before the destroying engines of the people of Columbia.

And Lawrence, and the brave men that fought under him, had honor and praise poured out upon them abundantly.

Moreover the people of New-York gave unto Lawrence vessels of silver, with curious devices; and they made a feast for the men who fought in the Hornet.

And all the people were exceedingly rejoiced at the valiant acts of Lawrence, and his fame extended throughout the land of Columbia; the sound of his name was the joy of the heart.

But when the news thereof reached the ears of the wise men of Britain, they said, Lo! these men are giants; neither are they like unto the warriors of the king.

And their witchcraft and their cunning are darkness unto us; even as when a man putteth a candle under a bushel.

Behold! five times hath the *"striped bunting"* of Columbia, triumphed over the royal cross of Britain.

Now the great Sanhedrim, who were assembled together, forgat not the valiant deeds of the mariners of Columbia.

For they divided amongst them more than seventy thousand pieces of silver.

And it came to pass, on the tenth day of the fourth month, in the same year, that the Chesapeake, a strong vessel of the United States, arrived in the haven of Boston.

She had sailed upon the face of the Tough waters more than an hundred days, after she departed from the land of Columbia, and passed a great way to the south:

And went hard by the island of Barbadoes, and those places, in the great sea, which encompass the world, from whence they bring poisoned waters, which open the womb of the earth to receive the unwary sons of men.

Moreover, in returning, she came nigh unto the Capes of Virginia, where the sweet scented plant[43] groweth in abundance.

And while she was on the ocean she captured a number of the vessels of the people of Britain, which were laden with rich merchandise.

---

[43] Tobacco

CHAP. XIX.

Capture of Little York, in Upper Canada— the destruction of the whole American army prevented by the precaution of Gen. Pike— his death.

Now, while these things happened in the south, and the evils of war destroyed the life of man, and the smiles of heaven strengthened the arms, and lifted up the glory of Columbia;

Behold, preparations of warfare were making on the borders of the great lakes of the north.

And the vessels of war of Columbia that were upon the waters of the lake called *Ontario*, were commanded by a brave man, whose name was *Chauncey*.

Now on the twenty fifth day of the fourth month, the army of Columbia, who were gathered on the shore of the lake, went down into the strong vessels of Chauncey.

And the number that went into the vessels was about two thousand.

And *Henry*[44] and *Zebulon*, whose sur-name was *Pike*,[45] were the chief captains of the host of Columbia.

On the same day the sails of the vessels were spread to the winds of heaven, and they moved towards a place called Little York,[46] in the province of Canada.

---

[44] Major General Dearborn.
[45] Brig. Gen. Pike.
[46] Capital of U. Canada.

Howbeit, the winds were adverse and blew with great violence from the east.

Nevertheless, on the morning of the twenty-seventh day of the same month, the army of Columbia, commanded by Pike, the chief captain, moved out of the strong ships of the United States.

But Henry remained on board the vessel of Chauncey, neither came he to the water's edge.

And the place where the host of Columbia landed was to the west of the town, about twenty and four furlongs, and from the strong hold of the king about ten furlongs.

The gallant Forsyth, who led a band of brave men, who fought not for filthy lucre's sake, went before the host.

And their weapons of war were of curious workmanship,[47] and they sent forth balls of lead; such as were unknown to Pharaoh when he followed the children of Israel down into the red sea.

Now Zebulon, with a thousand chosen men, followed close after *Forsyth*, the warrior.

About this time the savages and the servants of the king, even a great multitude, opened their engines of destruction without mercy.

And from the forest, and the secret places, their balls were showered like unto hail-stones, and the sound thereof was as sharp thunder.

And a man, whose name was *Sheaffe*, was the chief captain of the host of Britain.

---

[47] Rifles.

Now the destroying engines of the strong hold of the king issued fire and smoke with a mighty noise, and shot at the vessels of the United States.

But Chauncey returned unto them four-fold; and the battle waxed hot, both on the land and on the water.

And the men of Columbia rushed forward with fierceness, and drove the men of Britain from their strong hold.

So they fled towards the town for safety, for they were overcome; and the savages were smitten with fear, their loud yellings ceased, and their feet were light as the wild roe;

Nevertheless, the men of Columbia shouted aloud, and sounded their trumpets, their cymbals, and their noisy drums, which were contrived since the days of Jeroboam, king of Israel.

And Zebulon, the valiant warrior, followed hard after them; and they found no rest; for they were sore pushed, and the phantom of their imaginations pictured out new evils.

So when they found they were nigh being made captive, they departed in haste from the town and from the strong hold thereof, save about two score.

Now when the army of Britain was overthrown; when they were compelled to flee from the strong hold; the wickedness of Satan entered into their hearts.

And they gathered together abundance of the black dust and fixed it into the lowermost part of the fort, below the walls of stone.

After which they put a lighted match nigh to it, so that when the whole army of Columbia got into the hold, they might be destroyed.

But the Lord, who is good, even he who governeth the destinies of man, permitted it not.

Now when Zebulon and his army came out of the thick woods, in battle array, to go forth against the strong hold,

Lo! they saw not the host of Britain: but the eye of Zebulon was as the eye of an eagle, his strength as the lion, and his judgment as the wise:

So he stayed his men of war from rushing forward towards the place, lest they might be entrapped: and he caused them to move along the wood to the light and to the left.

About this time a stripling, from the south, with his weapon of war in his hand, ran up to Zebulon, and spake unto him, saying,

Behold! a man of Britain appeareth in the fort; suffer me, I pray thee, to slay him, for he is busied with the destroying engines:

But Zebulon said, Nay; we are yet a great way off.

And the young man entreated him a second time, saying, I beseech thee, let me step out before the host and slay him, lest the engine be let loose upon us; then Zebulon said unto him, Go.

So he ran out before the army and shot the man, and he fell to the earth; and it was about a furlong off, and the weight of the ball was about the weight of a shekel.

But as the young man returned to where the army stayed, behold! the black dust in the hold caught fire, and it rent the air with the noise of a thousand thunders:

And the whole army fell down upon their faces[48] to the earth; and the stones, and the fragments of rocks, were lifted high; and the falling thereof was terrible, even unto death.

Yea, it was dreadful as the mighty earthquake, which overturneth cities.

And the whole face of the earth round about, and the army of Zebulon, were over-shadowed with black smoke; so that, for a time, one man saw not another:

But when the heavy clouds of smoke passed away towards the west, behold the earth was covered with the killed and the wounded.

Alas! the sight was shocking to behold; as the deed was ignoble.

About two hundred men rose not: the stones had bruised them; the sharp rocks had fallen upon them:

They were wedged into the earth: their weapons of war were bent down into the ground with them; their feet were turned towards heaven; their limbs were lopped off.

But when those who escaped unhurt arose and looked around, they beheld not their chieftain; be had fallen to the earth.

A huge stone smote him upon the back, and two of his officers, (one of whom was the gallant *Fraser*,[49] raised him up and led him forth from the field of murder; the one on the one side, and the other on the other side.

---

[48] However strange this may appear, it is a fact that the concussion of the air produced that effect on nearly all who fronted the explosion.

[49] Major Fraser, son of Donald Fraser of New-York.

And as they led him away he turned his head around to his brave warriors, and said unto them, Go on: I will be with you soon! I am not slain.

The magic of his words gave joy to their hearts; for they loved him as they loved their own father.

And with resistless force his noble band rushed on, at the trumpet's sound, over the heaps of slain and wounded to glory, and to triumph!

And a swift messenger ran down unto Henry, with these words in his mouth, Lo! the right hand of our army is slain! its pride is gone! Zebulon has fallen!

Immediately Henry departed from the fleet, and came to the shore, and went up and led the host of Columbia to the town and took it.

Now the slain, the maimed and the captives of the host of Britain that day, were about a thousand fighting men:

And the loss of the men of Columbia was about three hundred slain and wounded.

And Henry, the chief captain, gave great honor to the captains under him, even *Scott*, and *Boyd*, and *Porter*, and all the brave men that fought that day.

Nevertheless, Sheaffe, the captain of the king, escaped with a handful of men, and the swift-footed savages: leaving behind him the insignia of *British mercy*!—a human scalp!

But the rejoicings of the people were mingled with deep sorrow; for the brave were slain in battle.

Oh! earth, how long shall thy inhabitants delight in warfare? when shall the old men cease to weep for their children?

Behold yon lonely widows; they weep for their husbands and their children; but they shall see their faces no more!

The fair daughters of Columbia sigh for the return of their beloved.

Seest thou those little ones? they fly to their disconsolate mother, they leap with joy at the name of father! but he shall never return!

Oh! that they had cast the black dust into the sea! then might not the children of men weep and wail.

Now on the next day, when the army of Zebulon gat the tidings that their captain was slain, the tears started in their eyes; they were mule, their hearts failed them; and they became as weak women.

Moreover, the United States made great lamentations over him; and the remembrance of his name shall live in the hearts of the people.

The eagle of Columbia dropt a feather from her wing, which the angel of brightness caught ere it fell to the earth, ascended to heaven, and recorded the name of *Pike*.

CHAP. XX.

Sketches of the History of America.

The voice of many years shall drop upon the children of men; and our children's children shall hearken unto it in the days to come.

The country of Columbia is a wide extended land, which reacheth from the north to the south, more than eight thousand miles; and the breadth thereof is about three thousand.

Moreover, the name of the country was called after the name of a great man, who was born in a place called *Genoa*; being in *Italia*, on the sea-coast.

His name was *Christopher*, sur-named *Columbus*.

As the righteous man struggleth against wickedness, so did he against ignorance and stupidity.

Nevertheless, it came to pass, in the fourteen hundred and ninety-second year of the Christian era, that he crossed the waters of the mighty deep, a thing that had never been known among the sons of men:

And the place where he landed was an island in the sea, nigh unto the continent of Columbia, called *San Salvador*; which, being interpreted, signifieth a place of safety.

And the place was inhabited by wild savages, and they were naked.

Now when the people heard that Columbus had found a new land, they were astonished beyond measure, for it was many thousand miles off;

moreover, some of them strove to rob him of the honor, and he was treated wrongfully.

But his name was lifted up above his enemies, and it shall not be lost.

Now the land of Columbia is a most plentiful land, yielding gold and silver, and brass and iron abundantly.

Likewise, all manner of creatures, and herbs and fruits of the earth,

From the red cherry, and the rosy peach of the north, to the lemon, and the golden orange of the south.

From the small insect, that cheateth the microscopic eye, to the huge mammoth that once moved on the borders of the river Hudson; on the great river Ohio; and even down to the country of Patagonia in the south.

Now the height of a mammoth is about seven cubits and an half, and the length thereof fourteen cubits; and the bones thereof being weighed were more than thirty thousand shekels; and the length of the tusks is more than six cubits.

It is more wonderful than the elephant; and the history thereof, is it not recorded in the book of *Jefferson*, the scribe?[50]

The fierce tiger and the spotted leopard dwell in the dark forests; and the swift-footed deer upon the mountains and high places.

Now the number of inhabitants that are spread over the whole continent, is more than an hundred million.

And the people of Columbia, who are independent of the tyrants of the earth, and who dwell between the great river which is called *Mississippi*, in the

---

[50] Jefferson's notes on Virginia.

south, and the province of *Canada*, in the north, being numbered, are about a thousand times ten thousand souls.[51]

The men are comely and noble, and cowardice hath forgot to light upon them: neither are they a superstitious people; they are peace-makers, they love the God of Israel, and worship him; and there are no idolaters amongst them.

The women are passing beautiful; they are like unto fresh lilies; their cheeks are like wild roses; their lips as a thread of scarlet; nature hath gifted them with Roman virtue and patriotism; and they have spread goodness with a plentiful hand.

Now it had happened in times past that the king of Britain had made war upon the people of Columbia, even forty years ago.

For the riches and prosperity of Columbia had become great, and the king coveted them.

And the war raged with the might of Britain, even in the heart of the land of Columbia, for about the space of seven years, when the army of Columbia became triumphant; neither could the power of Britain conquer the sons of liberty.

So those who remained of the armies of Britain returned home to the king, their master; and there was peace throughout the United States, and a covenant made between the nations.

But the names of the wise men of the great Sanhedrim, in those days, and the names of those who fought hard in battle, and spilt their blood in the cause of liberty, are they not written in the books of the chronicles of those days?

Now the fatness of the land of Columbia bringeth people from all nations to dwell therein.

---

[51] The last census, in 1810, stated the amount at about 8,000,000, the number may now probably be increased to 10,000,000.

The people of Columbia use no persuasion, the sacred cause of LIBERTY IS THE STAR ATTRACTION; and the time shall come when the eyes of all men shall be opened, and the earth shall rejoice.

Their laws are wholesome, for the people are the lawgivers, even as it was in the days of Cesar: but they know no kings.

Here the poor *Briton*, that flies from the blood-suckers of his country, findeth plenty.

The nationless *Gaul* fleeth here for safety from the wrath of a shallow king.

The persecuted *Hibernian* stealeth away, like a thief in the night, to behold the resting place of freedom.

Here the dull *German*, the jealous *Spaniard*, and the royal *Scot*, are all received with the open hand of hospitality.

CHAP. XXI.

Depredations in the Chesapeake—Havre-de-Grace burnt by the British under Adm. Cockburn—attack on Crany Island—Hampton taken by the British—Outrages.

Now it came to pass, that the mighty fleet of Britain, which was moving round about the great Bay of Chesapeake, committed much evil upon the shores thereof.

And they robbed those who were defenceless, and carried away their fatted cattle, their sheep, and all those things which they found, and put them into the strong ships of the king.

Moreover, they burned the dwellings of the helpless with fire, and they accounted it sport.

And the old men, the little children, and the women, yea the fair daughters of Columbia, were compelled to fly from the wickedness of barbarians.

Even the small villages that rose beautifully on the river side, became a prey unto them, and were consumed by the *mighty conquerors of Europe.*

They were like hungry wolves that are never satisfied; destruction and devastation marked their footsteps.

Now the ships of the king were commanded by a wicked man whose name was *Cockburn*.

And it was so that on the third day of the fifth month, in the thirty and seventh year of the independence of the people of Columbia,

Cockburn, sur-named the wicked, led forth a host of the savage men of Britain, against a pleasant village, called *Havre-de-Grace*, which lieth on the borders of the *Susquehanna*, a noble river; being in the state of *Maryland*,

Now there was none to defend the place, save one man, whose sur-name was *O'Neil*, who came from the land of *Hibernia*, and him they made captive.

And they came as the barbarians of the wilderness; fierceness was in their looks, cruelty was in their hearts.

To the dwelling houses they put the burning brand, and plundered the poor and needy without pity; such wickedness was not done even among the Philistines.

The women and children cried aloud, and fell down at the feet of the chief captain of the king: but, alas! his heart was like unto the heart of Pharaoh; he heard them hot.

However, it came to pass, the next day, when the *brave* Cockburn had collected his booty, and glutted his savage disposition, he departed.

And on the sixth day of the same month he went against other unprotected villages, which lie on the river *Sassafras*, called, *Frederickstown* and *Georgetown*, and burnt them also.

So did he return to his wickedness as a dog returneth to his vomit.

Now about this time the number of the strong ships of Britain were increased, and great multitudes of the soldiers of the king came with them to the waters of the Chesapeake.

And it came to pass, on the twenty-second day of the next month, that Cockburn, the chief captain of the ships of Britain, sayed to go against a small island, nigh unto *Norfolk*, in the state of *Virginia*, called in the vernacular tongue *Crany-Island*.

And the number of the men of Britain that went against the island was about five thousand; and they began to get upon the shore about the dawning of the day.

Near unto this place a few vessels of Columbia, commanded by the gallant *Cassin*, were hemmed in by about a score of the mighty ships of the king.

Now the fighting vessels under Cassin were mostly small, and were called *gunboats*, and they were little more than half a score in number.

Howbeit, but a few days before they went against the *Junon*,[52] a strong ship of Britain, and compelled her to depart from before the mouths of the destroying engines.

But the island was defenceless; and there came to protect it an hundred brave seamen from the gun-boats, and an hundred and fifty valiant men from the *Constellation*, a fighting ship of the United States.

And they brought the destroying engines with them, and they let them loose upon the vessels of the king, and upon the men who were landing upon the shore.

And the thundering noise thereof astonished the servants of the king; for they knew there was but a handful of men upon the island.

Moreover, Britain in her folly had invented a new instrument of destruction, which they called *Congreve Rockets*; and they threw them in great abundance.

But they were harmless as turtle doves, for they killed not a man.

---

[52] British frigate Junon.

Now the men of Columbia, with their handicraft, shot the balls of iron strait as an arrow from a bow, and thereby did much damage to the slaves of the king.

Inasmuch as they slew about two hundred of the men of Britain that day; and drove the host of them from the island.

So the mighty army of Britain fled in haste to the strong ships of the king for safety.

Now on the twenty-fifth day of the same month the army of Britain went against a village called *Hampton*, which lieth in the state of *Virginia*, and took it.

Howbeit, the little band of Columbia, commanded by *Crutchfield*, fought hard against them.

Nevertheless, they prevailed over him, and slew seven of his men, and wounded others, upon which he fled; for the men of Britain were like unto a swarm of locusts.

But the blood of two hundred royal slaves became a sacrifice to the wickedness of their leaders.

There is a time when truth may be uttered with pleasure; and the droppings thereof are like unto frankincense and myrrh.

But, alas! the hour hath passed away or it hath not yet come; she hath gone down into the vale of tears; yea, deep sorrow treadeth upon her heels.

Oh! Albion! that a veil might be cast over the transgressions of that day:

Thy wickedness shall be written with a pen of iron, and with the point of a diamond.

It was here, even in Hampton, that thy strength and thy majesty rose up against the poor the sick and the needy.

Instead of protecting the tender women, the fairest work of God; the life of the world; behold! what hast thou done?

See! the shrieking matron cast herself into the waters that she may escape thy brutal violence: but all in vain; her garments are torn from her; she becomes a prey to thy savage lust.

Not she alone, but her daughter, and her fair sisters, have fallen into thy unhallowed hands, and been defiled!

Oh, Britain! the voice of violated chastity riseth up against thee: the mark of the beast is printed in thy forehead:

Even the old and weak men became victims of thy barbarity; thy servants stripped the aged *Hope*, and buffeted him; with the points of their swords did they torment him.

Do the groans of the murdered *Kirby* creep into thine ears? go thou and repent of thine evil; and do so no more: the Lord God of hosts shall be thy judge.

The people of Columbia shall forgive thy crimes against them; but the remembrance thereof shall live coeval with time; neither shall they forget the name of *Cockburn*.

Even the sect of the tories despised him; the evils which he wrought caused many of them to turn aside and walk in the footsteps of the great Sanhedrim.

And thou, black Revenge! dreadful fiend! sleep within the precincts of Hampton: a strong seal is put upon thy sepulchre; the sons of Columbia shall not disturb thee.

When they pass by this ill-fated town, they shall step aside and weep; neither shall they enter the streets thereof, lest they awaken thee.

And woe unto the royal potentate, or the princely ruler, that shall presume to break the seal, or rouse thee from thy slumbers!

Thy waking will be as the waking of the hungry tiger, when he riseth up to refresh himself; retribution shall be obtained; and the heathen shall tremble.

CHAP. XXII.

Russian mediation—Bayard and Gallatin sail for St. Petersburgh—the British compelled to abandon the siege of Fort Meigs.

The lofty eagle cutteth the air with his wings, and moveth rapidly along; the fish of the deep glide swiftly through the waters; the timid deer bounds through the thick forests with wonderful speed:

But Imagination surpasseth them all; she rideth on the fleet winds; she holdeth a stream of lightning in her hand.

In an instant she flieth from the frozen mountains of *Zembla*, in the regions of the north, to the burning sands of *Africa*, in the torrid zone.

Now the sons of Columbia were peacemakers; neither did their footsteps follow after warfare.

(It is written in the holy scriptures, Blessed are the peace-makers, for they shall be called the children of God.)

So the great Sanhedrim of the people sent two of the wise men of Columbia, the one named *Gallatin* and the other *Bayard*, into a distant country:

Even unto the extensive country of *Russia*, that there they might meet the wise men of Britain, and heal the wounds of the nations, and make peace with one another.

But the people of Britain are a stiff-necked race, and they yielded not to the entreaties of the great Sanhedrim; therefore the war continued to rage.

So it came to pass, on the fifth day of the fifth month, in the pleasant season of the year; when the trees put forth their leaves and the air is perfumed with the sweet scent of flowers, and the blue violets bespread the green hillocks;

That *Harrison*, the chief captain, from the west, the brave warrior, who had entrenched himself in the strong hold of *Meigs*, nigh unto the river *Miami*, sallied forth against the savages and the slaves of Britain, that hemmed him in.

Now there were about a thousand soldiers of the king, and a thousand savages that had besieged the fort many days; and threw therein the balls of destruction, and strove to make captive the army of Columbia.

Nevertheless Harrison, and his gallant little band, fought hard against them, and drove them from before the strong hold with great slaughter.

Likewise, the slain of Columbia was about four score, besides the wounded.

Moreover, the chief captain gave great honor to Miller and all the captains and soldiers under him; even those called militia.

And the names of the states called *Ohio* and *Kentucky* were raised high, by the valiant acts of their sons that day.

CHAP XXIII.

Surrender of Fort George and Fort Erie to the Americans—gen. Brown drives the British from before Sackett's Harbor, with great loss—Gens. Winder and Chandler made prisoners at Forty-mile creek.

Now, on the twenty-seventh day of the same month, being thirty days after Zebulon had gone to sleep with his fathers,

Henry, whose sur-name was Dearborn, and *Lewis*,[53] the chief captains of the army of Columbia, and Chauncey the commander of the fleet of the United States, that moved on the waters of the great lake Ontario, essayed to go against Fort George and Fort Erie, in the province of the king

For they had previously concerted their plan and matured it; and taken on board the ships, the army of Columbia, and a number of the destroying engines.

And when the vessels of Chauncey came nigh unto the place, they let the destroying engines loose upon the fort, with a roaring noise.

In the meantime the army landed upon the shore, and went against the servants of the king.

And the men of Britain were frightened at the sound of the warring instruments that reached their camp, and they fled in dismay towards the strong hold of Queenstown.

---

[53] Gen. Morgan Lewis.

And they destroyed their tents, and their store-houses, and put a match to the black dust of their magazines, and blew them up into the air; this they did even from *Chippawa* and *Albino*.

Moreover, the slain and wounded of the king were two hundred two score and ten; of the men of Columbia about three score were slain and maimed.

So the forts George and Erie were captured by the army and navy of the United States.

And Henry, and Isaac, whose sur-name was Chauncey, spake well of all the captains and men that fought with them.

The gallant captains Scott and Forsyth fought bravely; neither were they afraid.

Boyd, and McComb, and Winder, and Chandler, and Porter, and a host of heroes, turned not aside from the heat of the battle.

And here the noble spirit of the youthful *Perry* burst forth into view; a man made to astonish the world, and shower down glory upon the arms of Columbia.

Now it happened about the same time that the strong ships of Britain moved towards the other end of the lake, to the east thereof, and went against the place called *Sackett's Harbor*.

The fleet of the king was commanded by a chief captain whose name was *Yeo*; and *Prevost*, the governor of Canada, commanded the army.

And on the morning of the twenty-ninth day of the month, they landed more than a thousand men on the shores of Columbia.

Howbeit, a certain valiant man, even *Jacob*, whose sur-name was *Brown*, commanded the host of Columbia that went against them:

And Jacob, albeit a man of peace,[54] drove the men of Britain, and compelled them to flee rapidly from the shore, and get them into their vessels.

So Prevost and Yeo returned to the strong hold of Kingston.

And the skill of Jacob, in driving away the soldiers of the king, pleased the people, and they honored him greatly.

Not many days after these things, there was a sore battle fought, near to a place called Forty-mile Creek.

And it was so that Winder and Chandler, two brave captains of the United States, and about four score men, were come upon unawares in the darkness of the night, and made captive by the servants of the king.

After which they were conveyed to the strong hold of Montreal, which lieth in the province of Canada, on the river St. Lawrence.

The officers and soldiers of Columbia fought bravely, and there were many slain and wounded on both sides;

Nevertheless, the army of the United States rested nigh unto the place.

---

[54] General Brown is a Quaker.

CHAP. XXIV.

Capture of the Chesapeake—Com. Decatur blockaded in New-London.

In these days the pride of Britain was sorely wounded; for she had been discomfited upon the waters of the great deep; and disappointment had sharpened her anger.

The people of Columbia had triumphed over her ships; and her mighty armies had gained no honors.

Notwithstanding she had made peace with the nations of Europe, and her whole strength was turned against the people of Columbia.

The prosperity of many hundred years had flattered her, and she was puffed up with the vanity thereof; yea, she had forgotten herself.

So it came to pass, on the first day of the sixth month, a certain strong ship of the king, called the *Shannon*, appeared before the haven of *Boston*, which lieth to the east.

And she bid defiance to the vessels of Columbia; for she had prepared herself for the event.

Now the *Chesapeake*, a fighting ship of the United States, was nigh unto the place; and she was commanded by the brave *Lawrence*, who had gained much honor in the sight of the people; neither was he afraid.

And he went forth to battle against, the vessel of the king, which was commanded by *Broke*, a valiant man.

Moreover, the mischievous engines that were in the ship of Britain were more, likewise the number of their men were greater than those of the vessel of the United States.

For Broke had gotten about two hundred men, and secreted them, so that when the hour of danger arrived they might assist his men, and fall unawares upon the men of Lawrence.

Nevertheless, towards the going down of the sun, the vessels drew nigh unto each other.

And Lawrence spake unto his officers and his mariners, saying:

Now shall we set our engines at the work of destruction; let the fire issue out of their mouths, as it were like unto fiery dragons.

And although their numbers be greater than ours, yet may we be conquerors; for he who is little of spirit gaineth nothing.

But if, peradventure, we should be overcome, even then shall not the sacred cause of LIBERTY perish, neither shall the people of Columbia be disheartened.

Also, your names shall be recorded as the champions of freedom.

And the. nations of the earth shall learn with astonishment, how dearly you prize the inheritance of your fathers.

Now when Lawrence had made an end of speaking, they sat the destroying engines to work, and rushed one upon another like fierce tigers.

The fire and smoke were abundant, and tremendous was the noise that floated upon the waters round about,

And the Chesapeake fell close upon the Shannon, swords clashed with swords, and pikes with pikes; and dreadful was the conflict thereof.

But the men of Broke were more numerous than the men of Lawrence, and overpowered them, by the means of their numbers.

Already had the valiant Lawrence fallen; his life-blood flowed fast; still he cried out to his brave companions, saying unto them, *Don't give up the ship*: his noble spirit fled, but his name shall not perish.

Moreover, about this time all the officers of the ship of the United States were either slain or sorely wounded; so she was captured by the vessel of the king.

After which the wickedness of barbarians again came forth; to be conquerors was not enough: but they were vain-glorious and overjoyed, and so became prodigal in spilling the blood of their prisoners.

Satan rose up in their hearts, and they shot the balls of death down into the hold of the vessel of the United States, even against the halt and maimed who had surrendered themselves.

And when the tidings thereof reached the kingdom of Great Britain, the lords, the princes, the rulers, yea, all the people were rejoiced beyond measure.

And they bid their roaring engines utter their voices, in London, their chief city, that had been silent many years, even those in the great tower,[55] which was built by William the conqueror, more than seven hundred years ago.

Their joy was unbounded, for they had overcome ONE of the strong ships of Columbia.

---

[55] On this occasion they fired their tower guns, which had not been done since Nelson's victory.

Now the slain and the wounded on board the Chesapeake, were an hundred two score and four; and there fell of the servants of the king about two hundred.

Amongst the slain of Columbia were also *Augustus*, whose sur-name was *Ludlow*, and another brave officer whose name was *White*.

And when the people of Columbia heard of a truth that Lawrence was slain, they mourned for him many days.

His body was conveyed to a place called *Halifax*, in the province of the king, where they honored his name, and buried him for a while.

But in process of time his body was taken out of the earth, likewise the body of Ludlow, and conveyed to the city of New-York.

And the captain's name who brought the bodies away from Halifax, was *Crownin-shield*.

So Lawrence was buried in the burial-place of his fathers, in his own land: and a great multitude of people went out to behold the funeral as it passed through the city.

And his valiant deeds shall live in the remembrance of the people.

About this time, on the fourth day of the month, the brave Decatur essayed to go forth with his vessels upon the waters of the mighty deep.

And the vessels that were with him were called the *United States*, the *Hornet*, and the *Macedonian*; a strong ship which he had captured from the king.

But it was so, that some large vessels of Britain, carrying each of them more than seventy of the destroying engines, suffered him not to go forth.

Moreover, they wished to retake the Macedonian, that they might retrieve the shame of the capture thereof.

So the ships of Britain blockaded Decatur and his ships in the haven of *New-London*, being in the latitude of *blue-lights*, which lieth in the state of *Connecticut*, nigh unto a place called *Stonington*, and they remained there many months.

CHAP. XXV.

Capture of Col. Boerstler and Major Chapin, with their command—treatment of prisoners —Major Chapin's escape.

Now there was much hard fighting on the borders, for the nations were wroth against one another, and many men were slain by the sword.

(But it is written in the book of Jeremiah the prophet, that, He who is slain by the sword, is better than he who is slain by famine.)

Nevertheless, many of the soldiers of Columbia suffered by the means thereof, for the cruelty of Britain hath not been exceeded by any.

Inasmuch, as they gave unto them who fell into their hands unwholesome food, and a scanty fare.

But when the servants of the king became captives to the people of Columbia, they were kindly treated, and partook of the fat of the land.

Now it came to pass, in the second year of the war, on the twenty-third day of the sixth month,

That a captain of the United States, whose sur-name was *Boerstler*, was ordered to go forth from the strong hold of Fort George, to annoy the enemy.

And the name of the place where he essayed to go, was called *Beaver-dams*, being distant from the strong hold of Queenstown about seventy furlongs.

And the number of the men of war of Columbia who followed after him was little more than five hundred.

But when they came nigh unto the place, early in the morning of the next day, lo! they were encompassed round about by the savages and soldiers of the king.

Nevertheless, they fought bravely for a time, and Dearborn, the chief captain of Fort George, sent the valiant Chrystie to help him out of his snare.

But Boerstler and his army had already become captive to the men of Britain.

And they made a covenant in writing, between one another, but the men of Britain violated the covenant.

Inasmuch as they permitted the savages to rob the officers of their swords, and their apparel, yea, even the shoes from off their feet.

After which the men of Columbia were commanded to go in boats, down to the strong hold of Kingston, in the province of the king.

But a certain brave captain, called *Chapin*, [56] a cunning man withal, made his escape in a boat, and arrived at the strong hold of Fort George; having, by the strength of his single arm, overpowered three of the strong men of Britain.

---

[56] Major Chapin.

CHAP. XXVI.

Capture of Fort Schlosser and Black Rock— Gen. Dearborn resigns his command to gen. Boyd) on account of sickness— six nations declare war against Canada.

And it came to pass, on the fourth day of the seventh month, which is the birth day of Columbian Liberty and Independence,

In the dark and solemn hour of the night, when the deadly savage walketh abroad, and the hungry wolves howl along the forest,

A band of the men of Britain crossed over the water from *Chippawa* to a place called *Fort Schlosser*,

And there was a handful of the men of the United States in the place, whom they made captive, being twelve in number.

Likewise, they carried away the bread and the meat, and some of the strong waters; also one of the destroying engines.

Moreover, the engine which they brought away was made partly of brass, partly of iron, and partly of wood.

And the weight of the ball that issued out of its mouth was about two hundred shekels, after the shekel of the sanctuary.

On the tenth day of the same month they also passed over the river Niagara, towards a place called *Black Rock*, and the small band at the place fled.

And they destroyed the strong house, and the camp with fire, and carried away the flour, and the salt, and such things as they stood in need of.

However, while they were yet carrying them away, there came a band of men of the United States, from the village of *Buffaloe*,

And let their instruments of war loose upon them; and smote them even unto death; albeit, those who were not slain escaped with their plunder.

And they fled hastily away, leaving nine of their slain behind, and more than half a score of captives.

The soldiers of the king were commanded by two men, the one called *Bishop* and the other *Warren*, and the men of Columbia were commanded by a chief captain, named *Porter*.[57]

About this time the savages and the men of war of Britain assailed the guards and the out-posts near unto Fort George.

Day after day and night after night did they annoy them; and many were slain on both sides.

And Dearborn, the chief captain of the fort, and of the host of Columbia round about Niagara, became sick and unable to go out to battle.

So *Boyd*, a brave and tried warrior, was made chief captain in his stead, until *Wilkinson*, the chief captain, arrived: and the gallant Fraser was appointed one of his aids.

Now there were some amongst the tribes of the savages, who had been instructed in the ways of God, and taught to walk in the path of righteousness;

For the chief governor of the land of Columbia, and the great Sanhedrim of the people, had taken them under their care,

---

[57] Gen. P. B. Porter.

And sent good men amongst them to preach the gospel, and instruct them in the sublime doctrine of the Saviour of the world.

And they hearkened unto the preachers, and were convinced, and their natures were softened.

Amongst these tribes were those who were called, the Six nations of New-York Indians:

And their eyes were opened, and they saw the evil and the wickedness of Britain.

So their chiefs and their counsellors rose up and made war against the province of Canada, and fought against the hired savages of the king of Britain.

But in all their acts they suffered not the spirit of barbarians to rule over them.

They remembered the good counsel given to them by their aged chief.[58]

And when the red savages and the men of Britain fell into their hands, they raised neither the tomahawk nor the scalping knife.

Nay, they treated them kindly; and those who were slain in battle they disturbed not; and their humanity exceeded the humanity of the white men of Britain.

---

[58] Alluding to an eloquent speech, delivered about that time, to the Six Nations, by one of their old warriors.

CHAP. XXVII.

Affairs on Lake Ontario, between the fleets of Com. Chauncey and Sir James Yeo.

In those days, the great waters of the lake *Ontario* were troubled with the movements of the fighting ships of Columbia, as well as those of the king.

Now the fleet of the king, which was commanded by *Yeo*, who was a skilful captain, was greater than the fleet of Columbia, which was commanded by the brave *Chauncey*.

And they had contrived to move to and fro upon the bosom of the lake Ontario many months,

And two of the small vessels, called the *Julia* and the *Growler*, being parted from the fleet, fell into the hands of Yeo.

Nevertheless, Chauncey followed after Yeo, and hemmed him in for a time.

But a strong west wind arose and the fleets were again separated.

After this Chauncey captured a number of small fighting vessels, and about three hundred soldiers of the king.

Now it was so, that when Yeo put his fleet in battle array, as though he would fight,

Then Chauncey went out against him, to meet him, and give him battle; but the heart of Yeo failed him, and he turned aside from the ships of Columbia.

So Chauncey sailed along the borders of the lake, from the one end to the other; even from Niagara to Sackett's Harbor, and Yeo followed him not.

Now all the vessels of the king, and all the vessels of the United States, that carried the destroying engines, upon the lake Ontario, being numbered were about seventeen.

Howsoever, they cut down the tall trees of the forest, and hewed them, and built many more strong vessels; although they had no gophar-wood amongst them in these days.

And they made stories to them, even to the third story, and they put windows in them, and they pitched them within and without with pitch; after the fashion of the ark.

And, lo! some of the ships which they built upon the lake, carried about an hundred of the engines of death.

And the weight of a ball which they vomited forth was about a thousand shekels.

Now the rest of the acts of Chauncey and Yeo which they did, are they not written in the book of *Palmer*, the scribe?[59]

---

[59] Historical Register, an excellent publication, in 4 vols. octavo, printed in Philadelphia, 1816; which contains the facts and the official documents of the late war.

CHAP. XXVIII.

Affairs on Lake Champlain—pillage of Plattsburgh by the British—bombardment of Burlington—depredations committed in the Chesapeake, and along the coast.

Now the fighting vessels of Britain began to appear upon the lake, called, by the ancient Gauls, *Champlain*.

And the vessels of war of Columbia that were upon the waters of the lake were not yet prepared for battle; the name of the commander whereof was *McDonough*, (a stripling).

So it came to pass, on the thirty and first day of the seventh month, that the vessels of the king came forward against *Plattsburgh*, which lieth on the borders of the lake.

And there were none to defend the place; for the army of *Hampton*, a chief captain of the United States, was encamped upon the opposite side of the lake, at a place called *Burlington*, in the state of *Vermont*.

And the number of the soldiers of the king that landed at Plattsburgh was more than a thousand men, and the name of their chief captain was *Murray*.

And a captain of the United States, whose name was *Mooers*, a man of valor, strove to gather together the husbandmen of the place, but they were not enough.

So the army of the king captured the place; and the men of Columbia fled before the men of war of Britain.

Moreover, the wickedness which had been committed at *Hampton*, was noised abroad, even from the shores of Virginia to lake Champlain.

Accordingly all the women and children. who were able, suddenly departed from the place, lest the same thing might, peradventure, happen unto them.

Neither were they deceived in judgment; for, lo! when the place was given up, and a covenant made, the servants of the king proved faithless.

They abided not by the contract; saying, Pish! ye are but Yankees, therefore will we do to you as seemeth meet unto us!

So they burnt the houses, and all other things belonging to the United States, with fire.

After which they fell upon the merchandise, the goods, and the chatties of all manner of persons; nay, the persons of some of the women were abused:

Meanwhile they forced others to put the burning brand to their own dwellings; or pay them tribute.

They killed the cattle, and prepared them food; and after they had eaten and drank, they overturned the tables.

So when their vengeance was completed, they departed to other places and committed like evils.

About the same time the vessels of the king, that sailed on the lake, went against the town of Burlington; where the army of Hampton was.

But when the men of Columbia began to let the destroying engines loose upon them from the strong hold before the town, they fled in dismay.

Now while these things were passing in the north, the greedy sons of Britain were laying desolate the small villages of the south.

On the waters of the Chesapeake they captured the small vessels and made spoil thereof.

Moreover, they gat possession of a Small place called *Kent Island*, and robbed the poor and needy; for there was no mercy in them.

Yea, it was said of a truth, and talked abroad, that they came in the night time, and disturbed the small cattle, and the fowls, and took them for their own use, and crawled away like men ashamed;

Thus committing a sin, by violating the eighth commandmant of God, which saith, THOU SHALT NOT STEAL.

Even the state of *North-Carolina* escaped them not; they landed a thousand men of war at a place called *Ocracocke*.

And again the work of destruction began; they spread terror and dismay whithersoever they went.

They troubled the men of Columbia all along the sea coast, which is more than eight thousand furlongs, from north to south.

Moreover, they gat much plunder; even much of the good things with which the land of Columbia aboundeth.

CHAP. XXIX.

Major Croghan defeats the British and Indians, under Gen. Proctor, in their attack on fort Stephenson, Lower Sandusky.

Nevertheless, it came to pass, that Harrison, the chief captain of the north west army, had placed a captain, a young man, in the hold called *Fort Stephenson*, to defend it.

Now the fort lieth at the western end of the great lake Erie, at a place called *Sandusky*.

And the number of the soldiers that were with the youth in the hold, was about an hundred and three score, and they had only one of the destroying engines.

Now the name of the young man was *George*, and his sur-name was *Croghan*.

So on the first day of the eighth month, about the going down of the sun, a mighty host from Malden appeared before the hold.

Even a thousand savages, and about five hundred men of war of Britain; and *Proctor* was the commander thereof.

Moreover, they brought the instruments of destruction in great plenty; even *howitzers*, which were not known in the days of the children of Israel.

And they had prepared themselves for the fight, and encompassed the place round about, both by land and by water.

After which Proctor sent a message to the brave Croghan, by a captain whose name was *Elliot,* and the words thereof were in this sort:

Lo! now ye can neither move to the right nor to the left, to escape, for we have hemmed you in;

Therefore, that your blood may not be spilt in vain, we. command that ye give up the strong hold into the hands of the servants of the king, and become captives.

We have the destroying engines in abundance, and we are a numerous host.

Furthermore, if ye refuse then shall the wild savages be let loose upon you; and there shall be none left among you to go and tell the tidings thereof.

But when Croghan heard the message, he answered and said unto Elliot, Get thee now to thy chief captain, and say unto him, I refuse; neither will I hearken unto him:

And if it be so, that he come against me with his whole host, even then will I not turn aside from the fierce battle; though his numbers were as the sand on the sea shore.

Lo! David, of old, with a sling and a stone slew the mighty Goliah: and shall the people of Columbia be afraid, and how before the tyrants of Europe?

Then Elliot returned to the army of the king; and immediately the mouths of their engines were opened against the fort.

And the noise thereof continued a long time; even until the next day; but their battering prevailed not.

Now when Proctor saw it was of no avail, he divided his host into two bands, and appointed a captain to each band; and they moved towards the fort and assailed it with great violence.

But the men of Croghan were prepared for them; and they let loose their weapons of war upon them, and set their destroying engine to work, and smote the men of Britain, hip and thigh, with great slaughter.

And the deep ditch that surrounded the fort was strewn with their slain and their wounded.

So the host of Britain were dismayed and overthrown, and fled in confusion from the fort into the forest; from whence, in the dead of the night, they went into their vessels, and departed from the place.

Now the loss of the men of Britain was about an hundred two score and ten; and of the men of Columbia there was one slain and seven wounded.

But when Proctor had rested his army he sent a skilful physician to heal the maimed which he had fled from and left behind.

But Harrison, the chief captain said unto him, Already have my physicians bound up their wounds, and given them bread and wine, and comforted them; after the manner of our country.

For we suffer not the captives that fall into our hands to be buffeted or maltreated; neither want they for any thing.

So the physician of the king's army was permitted to return to his own camp.

Moreover, great honor and praise were bestowed upon the brave Croghan, the captain of the fort, for his valiant deeds; and his name was spoken of with joy throughout the land of Columbia.

CHAP. XXX.

British Schooner Dominica; of 14 Guns, Captured by the privateer Decatur, Of 7 Guns— U. S. brig Argus captured by the Pelican— capture of the Boxer by the U. S. brig Enterprise,

---

Now the war continued to rage without abatement upon the waters of the great deep;

And manifold were the evils that came upon the children of men by the means thereof.

Moreover, the great Sanhedrim of the people were forced to bestir themselves; and they had continued their councils day after day without ceasing.

And it came to pass, that there was a dreadful battle fought between a vessel of the king, and a private vessel of Columbia.

Now the name of the vessel that fought was *Decatur*, and the captain's name was *Diron*, a Gaul.

And it was so, that about the fourth day of the eighth month, the Decatur having sailed out of the haven of *Charleston*, being in the state of *South Carolina*, fell in with one of the fighting vessels of the king, called the *Dominica*.

But the destroying engines of the king's vessel were two-fold greater in numbers than those of the Decatur.

Nevertheless, they set them to work, so that they groaned beneath the fire and smoke;

And in about the space of an hour the Dominica was conquered and taken captive.

For when the vessels came close together, the men smote one another with their swords and weapons of war; yea, even the balls of iron they cast at each other, with their hands, and slew one another with wonderful slaughter.

Inasmuch as there were slain and maimed of the king three score souls; those of the Decatur were about a score: moreover the captain of the Dominica was slain.

The fight was an unequal one; and the bravery of Diron gained him a great name, for he overcame the enemies of freedom; although their force was greater than his.

After this, on the fourteenth day of the same month, there was another sore battle between a small vessel of the United States, called the *Argus*, and the *Pelican*, a ship of the king.

Now the Pelican was somewhat stronger than the Argus, and they were stubborn and kept the destroying engines to work, with great noise, about forty and five minutes.

And the brave captain of the Argus, whose name was *Allen*, was wounded unto death, and the vessel of Columbia was captured by the ship of Britain, the name of the commander whereof was *Maples*.

Of the men of Columbia six were slain and seventeen wounded; of the men of Britain the slain and wounded were five.

Now the death of Allen was spoken of with sorrow throughout the land of Columbia, for he had defended the vessel of the United States nobly: and captured some merchant ships of Britain.

Even the enemy regarded him for his bravery, for they buried him with honor in their own country, not far from the place where he became captive, which was in the waters of the king, even in St. George's Channel.

But it came to pass, on the fifth day of the next month, in the same year,

That a certain small vessel of Columbia, carrying the engines of destruction, commanded by a gallant man, whose name was *Burrows*, fell in with another small vessel of the king, called the *Boxer*, and the captain thereof was a brave man, and his name was *Blythe*.

In the language of the people of the land, the vessel of Columbia was called the *Enterprize*.

Now when the vessels drew nigh unto each other the men shouted with loud shouting.

And immediately they let the mischievous engines loose upon one another, with a noise like unto thunder.

But it happened, that in about the space of forty minutes, the Boxer was overcome; but she was taken somewhat unawares:

For, lo! the pride of the men of Britain had made them foolish; and, thinking of conquest, they nailed Britannia's red-cross to the mast of the vessel.

Whereupon, after they were overcome, they cried aloud for mercy, saying,

Behold! our colors are fast; and we cannot quickly unloose them: nevertheless, we will be prisoners unto you, therefore spare us.

So the brave mariners of Columbia spared them, and stopped the destroying engines; for their hearts were inclined to mercy.

However, this was another bloody fight; for there fell of the men of Britain forty that were slain outright, and seventeen were wounded.

And the loss of Columbia in slain and maimed was about fourteen.

And the commanders of both vessels were slain; and they buried them With honor in the town of *Portland*, which leaveth *Boston* to the west; for the battle was fought hard by.

Moreover, the great Sanhedrim was pleased with the thing, and gave unto the kinsman of Burrows a medal of gold, in token of remembrance thereof.[60]

---

[60] Mathew L. Davis, of New-York, passing by and observing the burial place of Burrows, stopt and ordered a monument to be erected to his memory at his own private expense.

CHAP. XXXI.

The capture of the British Fleet on Lake Erie, by the American fleet under Com. Perry.

The Lord, in the plenitude of his wisdom and power, ordaineth all things which come to pass: and the doings are for the benefit of man, and for the glory of God.

For where is the evil which hath not turned to an advantage, and been a warning, and swallowed up the evil that might have come?

Now about this time the strong vessels of Columbia, that moved upon the face of the blue waters of the great lake *Erie*, were given in charge to *Oliver*, whose sur-name was *Perry*.

And he was a prudent man, and had prepared himself to meet the vessels of the king, even forty days before hand.

And the name of the captain of the fleet of Britain was *Barclay*, a man of great valor; but he boasted and was vain of his fleet, for it was more powerful than the fleet of Columbia.

Nevertheless, it came to pass, in the one thousand eight hundred and thirteenth year, on the tenth day of the ninth month, early

The valiant Perry beheld the fleet of the king at a distance upon the lake; so he unmoored his vessel and went out to meet them in battle array, fleet against fleet.

And when their white sails were spread upon the bosom of the lake, they appeared like unto a squadron of passing clouds.

A gentle breeze wafted the hostile vessels towards one another.

It was silence upon the waters; save when the sound of musical instruments fell sweetly upon the ear.

But it happened, a little before the mid-day, that the shouts of the men of war of Britain were heard, and the shouts of the men of Columbia.

And now the destroying engines began to utter their thunders, vomiting forth fire and smoke and brimstone in abundance.

And suddenly the waters were in an uproar; and the bellowing noise sounded along the lake.

Moreover, the chief force of the ships of the king was put against the vessel in

And the vessel was called the *Lawrence*, after a brave man, whose dying words waved upon her, aloft:

Now, behold, a thousand balls of iron skim the surface of the waters, swift as shooting stars.

Perry saw that the tackling of his vessel was shot away, and his men were slain and wounded with great slaughter, and his destroying engines became silent,

He put the charge of the vessel into the hands of one of his officers, whose name was *Yarnell*, a trusty man:

Then, with the starry banner of Columbia in his hand, did the gallant Perry leap into his *cock-boat*, while his brave mariners quickly conveyed him to another fighting vessel of the United States, called the Niagara, commanded by a valiant man whose name was *Elliot*.

After this again the vessels uttered their thunders and fought hard, and the men of Columbia poured out destruction upon the servants of the king.

And it came to pass, that the skilful contrivance of Perry, and the bravery of his men, at length forced the whole fleet of the king to become captive, even unto the *cock-boats* of Columbia.

Thus again was the mighty lion humbled before the eagle: for six strong vessels of Britain were overcome at one time.

And the slain and wounded of the king that day, was an hundred thirty and five; besides there were about a thousand prisoners.

The loss of the United States was twenty and seven that were killed, and four score and ten were wounded.

Moreover, the number of the men of Britain made captive was more than all the men of Perry's squadron.

Now Perry was a righteous man, and, like the good Samaritan, took care of the halt and maimed, and put skilful men to bind up their wounds; and the men of Britain blessed him.

Neither was he a man puffed up with vanity, even in the hour of victory:

For when he had *conquered the fleet of Britain*, he wrote to *Jones*,[61] one of the scribes of the great Sanhedrim, with modesty, saying,

To day it hath pleased the Lord that the people of Columbia should triumph over their enemies.

---

[61] W. Jones, Secretary of the Navy.

At the same time he wrote to Harrison, the chief captain of the host of Columbia, whose army was at the bay of Sandusky, saying, *We have met the enemy, and they are ours!*

Then did the enemies of Columbia weep; and the gainsayer put on deep mourning.

Moreover, the great Sanhedrim honored Perry with great honor; yea, they thanked him, and gave him medals, with devices curiously wrought.

Likewise, the people gave him much silver plate, with gravings thereon, mentioning his deeds.

And the bye-stander might read his triumph in his country's eyes.

His sons shall hear him spoken of with pleasure; and his name shall be mentioned in the song of the virgins.

Where, oh! Albion, are now thy mighty admirals? where thy Nelson? where the transcendant glory they gained for thee?

Alas! it hath expired upon the waters of Erie, before the destroying engines of Perry!

CHAP. XXXII.

Capture of Malden and Detroit—the army of Gen. Proctor retreat towards the Moravian towns—Gen. Harrison pursues them.

Now when Perry had taken care of the captives, and the wounded, and set them upon the shore,

He began to convey the army of Harrison from Fort Meigs and round about.

And having gathered them together into his vessels, he brought them, and landed them nigh unto the strong hold of Malden.

And it came to pass, on the twenty-third day of the same month, in which Perry conquered the fleet of Britain,

That Harrison, the chief captain, began to march the host of Columbia against the strong hold of Malden, and captured a town called *Amherstburgh*, nigh thereunto.

Now Proctor was the chief captain of the savages and servants of the king.

And when he saw the men of Columbia approach, he destroyed the fort, the tents, and the store-houses of the king, and, with his whole host, fled swiftly towards Sandwich.

And Harrison, and the host of Columbia, followed hard after him.

Now when the savages of the wilderness beheld the men of Britain flee before the children of Columbia, their spirits sunk, and they were sore amazed.[62]

Moreover, they upbraided the servants of the king, saying, Lo! ye have deceived us, and led us from our hunting grounds, and we are an hungered:

For, verily, ye promised us bread and wine,[63] and silver and gold; yea, even that we should drink of the strong waters of Jamaica, if we would go out with you and fight the battles of the king, against the men of Columbia.

But, behold! now ye would run away and leave us to fight alone.

Whereupon many of their tribes cast away their tomahawks, and refused to fight under the banners of the king.

And when Harrison came to Sandwich, Proctor and his army had departed from the place, and fled towards the river *Thames*, near *Moravian Town*,

(Now the Thames emptieth its waters into the lake *St. Clair*, and the Moravian Towns lie upon the river, about an hundred miles from Malden, towards the north in the province of Upper Canada.)

Moreover, as they journied on, the brave *McArthur* crossed over with his band to the strong hold of Detroit, and took it.

But the savages and the men of Britain had destroyed those things which they could not carry away, and fled in haste.

So McArthur, in whom the chief captain put much faith, remained at Detroit in the charge thereof.

---

[62] See Tecumseh's letter to Proctor.

[63] At this time it will be remembered the British army were short of supplies.

And it came to pass, when Harrison saw that the host of Britain fled before him, he departed from Sandwich and went after them; it being on the second day of the next month.

And his whole army followed after him, in all about three thousand brave men from the back-woods of the state of *Kentucky* and the pleasant villages of *Ohio*.

Now Harrison was a mighty man of valor, and no man could make him afraid; and the captains and officers that were with him were all valiant men.

And, when some of his captains said unto him, Lo! there is a feast to-day; go thou and partake thereof, and refresh thyself, and we will watch;

He answered and said unto them, Nay, shall I go and riot, whilst the warriors of Columbia lie on the frozen ground?

No, their fate shall be my fate; and their glory shall be my glory.

So he wrapped himself in his cloak, and lay down in his own tent.

And the husbandmen of Kentucky were led on by their valiant governor, whose name was *Shelby*, and he was a man well stricken in years; even at the age of three-score did he go out against the enemies of Columbia; and all the people rejoiced in him.

And the gallant Perry staid hot behind; but freely offered his strength, and was one of the right hand men of Harrison, with whom he followed after the host of Britain.

Nevertheless, it happened that a band of the savages strove to give hindrance to the army of Columbia.

But the men of Columbia let two of the destroying engines loose upon them, and they fled into the wilderness like wild deer.

CHAP. XXXIII.

Battle of the Thames—Gen. Harrison captures the British army under Gen. Proctor—illuminations on account of it—news of it received in England.

And it came to pass, on the fifth day of the same month, that Proctor, with the savages and the army of the king, rested upon advantageous ground, on the banks of the river *Thames*,

Where he drew his army up in the order of battle, after the fashion of these days, and prepared himself to meet the host of Columbia.

Now the army of Proctor was mighty; for he had a thousand horsemen: but the number of the savages that followed after him are not known to this time; howbeit, they were many.

And they were under the charge of a chief warrior, whom they called *Tecumseh*, a savage whom the, king had made a chief captain.[64]

And it came to pass, on the same, day, in the latter part of the day, the army of Harrison drew nigh unto the place.

And he called together his captains of fifties, and. his squadrons, and encouraged them, and commanded them to prepare themselves for the fight.

And he put the host of Columbia in battle array against the host of Britain, army against army.

---

[64] Brig. General.

Now the sound of the trumpet, the cymbal, the bugle-horn, and the noisy drum, echoed through the deep wilderness.

And the red savages appeared in the field before the men of Britain, for they had put them, as a shield, in the front of the battle.

And they yelled with dreadful yellings, and sounded aloud the *war-whoop*, which was the signal of death.

But the army of Columbia rushed upon them with the fierceness of lions.

And the weapons of war were used without mercy; the foxes and the beavers crept into their holes, for the destroying engines frightened the wild beasts, so that they looked for their hiding places.

The gallant *Johnson*[65] fell upon them with a band of chosen horsemen, and he drove them before him like chaff before the wind, and smote their chief warrior,[66] and slew him with his own hand, so that he fell to the earth.

And the host of Columbia assailed the men of Britain on all sides, and overcame them and made them prisoners of war; whereupon the engines ceased to utter their thunders.

Howbeit, Proctor escaped, on a swift running horse, with a handful of his captains that were under him.

Now the number of prisoners captured by the army of Harison that day were about six hundred.

And the slain and wounded of the men of Britain were thirty and three; and the same number of savages were slain.

---

[65] Col. Johnson, of the Kentucky light-horse.
[66] Tecumseh; who was at that moment in the act of shooting the colonel.

Of the army of Columbia seven were slain and two score and two were wounded.

But the men of Kentucky and Ohio, whose sons and brothers and fathers had been inhumanly slaughtered at the River Raisin, slew not a single captive.

But they treated them as men; thus doing good for evil; according to the word of the Lord.

Moreover, they captured six of the destroying engines that were made of brass, and two that were made of iron; besides many weapons of war.

Now three of the brass engines were those given to the men of Britain, at the capture of Detroit, the first year of the war, and were the same that had been taken from the king in the days of Washington.

Soon after the battle, Harrison returned with his army to Detroit, where many of the savages had assembled, to repent of their evils, and ask for mercy from the chief captain.

So Harrison made a covenant with them, and they were thankful, and gave him hostages.

Now there were great rejoicings among the children of Columbia, and the hearts of the people of the United States were exceeding glad.

So that when the news thereof reached them they drank wine; and when the evening came they lighted their candles, and put them in candlesticks of silver and candlesticks of gold.

And there were many thousands of them; and the light thereof was as though the stars had fallen from heaven.

This did they throughout the land of Columbia, from the district of *Maine*, in the east, to the state of *Georgia*, in the south.

But the sect of the tories shut their eyes; neither would they go out to behold the glory of the light thereof.

Moreover, when the *Prince Regent*, and the chief counsellors, and the wise men of Britain, heard the tidings, for a truth, that their fleet and their army were captured, they were astonished beyond measure.

They looked at one another like men who had lost their wits: they were silent, and their tongues clave to the roof of their mouths.

Their knees smote one against another, for the strength of Britain was shaken; her valiant warriors lost their honor;[67] and her glory was outshone.

Now there were great honor and praise bestowed upon Harrison for his courage, and his valiant acts; and the people remembered his name with pleasure.

Moreover, he gave great praise to Shelby, the governor, and Perry, and Johnson, and all the brave men that were with him.

And in the same month, when the object of the army was fulfilled, the husbandmen of Columbia returned every man to his own house.

But Harrison and Perry, and the band of warriors of the great Sanhedrim, went into their vessels.

And they moved from *Detroit* and came in the ships of Perry to *Buffalo*, nigh unto the river *Niagara*, to meet *Wilkinson*, who came from the south, and was appointed chief captain of the army of the centre.

---

[67] Doubly lost it: by water and by land; by being conquered and by being cruel.

CHAP. XXXIV.

War with the creek nation of Indians—massacre of fort Mimms—Georgia and Tennessee militia, under General Jackson, retaliate.

Now it came to pass, while these things were going on in the north, and the repentant savages laid their murderous weapons at the feet of Harrison,

That the servants of the king were stirring up the spirit of Satan in the savages of the wilderness of the south;

And placing the destroying engines into their hands that they might drink the blood of the people of Columbia.

Now those southern barbarians were called the *Creek nation of Indians*.

Moreover, they were a nation of savages that dwelt in the back-woods and the wilderness round about the states of *Georgia, Tennessee*, and the *Mississippi Territory*,

So about this time they took their weapons of death in their hands, and went against the strong hold of *Fort Mimms*, which lieth on a branch of the river *Mobile*, which emptieth its waters into the great *Gulf of Mexico*.

And they captured the place; and with the fury of demons they murdered, with the tomahawk, the men, the women, and the infants that were in and about the fort, sparing neither age nor sex; and slaying the prisoners that begged for mercy.

And the number of the people of Columbia that were massacred and burnt alive in their houses, that day, was about four hundred; however, there were an hundred savages slain.

For it was a sore fight; and *Beasley*, who commanded the fort, fought hard against them; howbeit, he was slain.

But it came to pass, in the same year, that the people of Columbia were revenged of the evil:

Andrew, whose sur-name was *Jackson*, a man of courage and valor, was chief captain in the south,

And he sent out one of his brave captains, whose name was *Coffee*, with a strong band; even nine hundred mighty horsemen:

Now these were the valiant husbandmen of *Georgia* and the back-woods of *Tennessee*; their horses were fleet as the roebuck; their weapons of war were certain death.

So they went forth against a town of the savages called *Tallushatches*, on the second day of the eleventh month.

And on the next day they encompassed the town round about; and the savages prepared themselves for battle.

About the rising of the sun they sounded their drums, and began their horrible yellings.

But they frightened not the hearts of the brave men of Tennessee.

So when Coffee had stationed his captains and his men of war about the town, in the order of battle, the whole army shouted aloud;

And the instruments of destruction were let loose upon them on all sides; and they fought with all their might.

But the men of Columbia rushed upon them, and subdued them, and made about four score women and children captive.

And slew about two hundred of their warriors; leaving not a man to tell the tidings.

For, lo! when the savages of the wilderness commit great evils and transgressions against the people of Columbia,

The great Sanhedrim of the people send out mighty armies against them, that are able to overthrow them, and make their towns a desolation, and lay waste their habitations.

Now the loss of the army of Columbia that day, was five slain and about forty wounded.

And Jackson, the chief captain, gave great praise to Coffee, and all the valiant men that fought that day.

On the next day after the battle, the army of Columbia returned to their camp, at a place called the *Ten-Islands*.

CHAP. XXXV.

Continuation of the war with the Creeks—Gen. Jackson's grand victory over them—they sue for peace—a treaty is concluded with them.

Notwithstanding their discomfiture, the nation of the Creeks were still bent on warring against the people of Columbia.

And they committed many outrages upon the inhabitants of the states round about.

But it came to pass, on the seventh day of the same month, that a messenger came to Jackson, the chief captain, and spake unto him, saying:

Lo! even now, more than a thousand savages have pitched their tents at *Talledoga*, near the strong hold of *Lashley*, with intent to assail it.

Immediately Jackson took two thousand hardy men, who were called *volunteers*, because they fought freely for their country, and led them against the savages.

Now the men of war that followed after him were mostly from the state of Tennessee, and men of dauntless courage.

So, early in the morning of the next day, the army of Jackson drew nigh the place, in battle array.

And the savages came out towards the army of Columbia, with shouting and yellings: and again the engines of destruction were used plentifully.

And the leaden balls whizzed about their ears like unto a nest of hornets.

But the horsemen, and the whole army of Jackson, rushed upon the savages, and slew them with great slaughter, and overcame them.

And the number of savages slain that day was about three hundred; and a red-cross banner of the Spanish nation was found amongst them and taken.

Seventeen of the men of Columbia were slain, and about four score wounded.

So, when the battle was over, Jackson returned to his own camp.

After these things had come to pass, on the twelfth day of the month, a certain captain, whose sur-name was *White*, was sent against another place called the *Hillabee-Towns*,

And, on the eighteenth day of the same month, he took the towns, and destroyed them, and slew three score of the savages, and made about two hundred two score and ten prisoners.

About eleven days afterwards, a valiant captain, whose name was *Floyd*, with his brave men, went against the towns of *Autossee* and *Tallisee*, which lie on the banks of the river *Tallapoosie*.

And Floyd went against them with boldness, and triumphed over them, and killed about two hundred of them, and burned their towns with fire, and slew the king of Autossee, and the king of Tallisee, who were the kings of two tribes.

Moreover, on the thirteenth day of the next month, *Claiborne*, a governor, and a man of valor, went against the savages that dwelt on the river *Alabama*;

And he marched with his army through the wilderness more than an hundred miles, to a town built upon a place called by the savages the *Holyground*, where three of the Indian prophets dwelt.

Now there were lying prophets among the savages, even as there were in the days of old; and they prophesied according to their own wishes;

And those of shallow understanding believed them, and were led into a snare, whereby their whole tribe was nigh being destroyed.

And *Wetherford*, the chief warrior of the Creek nation, was there also with his band.

And he fought hard against Claiborne; but he was overthrown, and fled, and the town was burnt, even two hundred houses.

After all these tribulations, the depredations of the savages of the south were not stayed.

So Jackson, the chief captain, went out against them with his army, and attacked them at their strong hold on the waters of the Tallapoosie, where they were entrenched, having more than a thousand warriors.

Now this was on the twenty and seventh day of the third month, in the one thousand eight hundred and fourteenth year of the age of Christianity.

And Jackson set his destroying engines to work, and fought desperately against them, for about the space of five hours; when he overcame them, so that only about a score escaped.

Seven hundred and fifty of the savage warriors were found slain in battle; and two hundred two score and ten women and children became captives to the army of Columbia.

Manahoee, their chief prophet, was smitten in the mouth, and slain, and two other false prophets were slain with him.

Moreover, about the first day of the sixth month, a brave man, whose name was *Pearson*, with the husbandmen of the states of *North* and *South Carolina*, went against them along the borders of the Alabama, and captured about six hundred of them.

Thus did the men of Columbia triumph over them, and conquer them, even to the seventh time.

And so the judgment of the Lord fell upon them for their unrighteousness, and for their wicked and murderous deeds.

After which they repented of their evil, having, through their own folly, lost many thousand warriors.

And the chief warriors gave up their instruments of destruction, and laid them at the feet of Jackson, the chief captain.

Even *Wetherford*, the chief warrior, gave himself up to Jackson, saying, I fought with my might; but I have brought evil upon my nation; and thou hast slain my warriors; and I am overcome.

Now the savages are easily inflamed and roused to works of sin and death; and of their weakness the servants of the king are not ashamed to take advantage; even to the ruin of the poor and ignorant barbarians.

So the warriors and the whole nation of the Creeks, being tired of a destructive war, entreated the men of Columbia for peace, saying unto Jackson,

Lo! now are our eyes opened to our own profit; now will we make peace with you.

And if ye will no more suffer the fire, and the sword, and the destroying engines to spread desolation amongst us,

Then will we make a covenant with you, and give you for an inheritance a great part of the land which our fathers inherited before us.

And the length and the breadth thereof shall be about as large as the whole island of Britain, whose men of war have led us into this snare.

For although the king, who calleth himself our father, across the great waters, did put the instruments of death into our hands, and give us the black dust in abundance; nevertheless he deceived us: and in the hour of danger his servants left us to take care of ourselves.

So Jackson made a covenant with them, and it was signed by the chiefs of their nation.

And after it had been examined by the wise men and the great Sanhedrim of the people, it was signed with the hand-writing of James, the chief governor of the land of Columbia.

CHAP. XXXVI.

Plan of attack on Montreal defeated.

The frailty of man speaketh volumes: one man accuseth another; but where is he who is perfect?

Man deviseth mighty plans in his own mind, but he accomplisheth them not.

He is wise in his own conceit, but his wisdom faileth him: he seeth folly in others, but perceiveth not his own; he is as a reed shaken with the wind.

Now the country of Columbia was assailed on every side by the enemies of freedom.

And in the hope that the war might speedily cease, and an end be made of the shedding of blood, the great Sanhedrim of the people wished to push their armies into the heart of the provinces of the king, even to *Montreal*.

So they pitched upon certain chief captains, who were well skilled in the arts of warfare; and *Wilkinson* and *Hampton* were the names of the captains;

And *Brown*, and *Boyd*, and *Covington*, and *Swift*, and *Coles*, and *Purdy*, and *Ripley*, and *Swartwout*, and *Fraser*, and many others, were valiant captains under them.

Not many days after Harrison returned from his triumph over Proctor's army; and in the same year, it came to pass that Wilkinson conveyed his army from Fort George and the country of Niagara, to Sackett's Harbor, at the east end of lake Ontario; leaving Harrison and *McClure* behind, at the strong hold of Fort George.

From Sackett's Harbor Wilkinson moved to a place called *Grenadier Island*; and in the first week of the eleventh month he arrived at Ogdensburgh, in order to go against the strong hold of Montreal.

Now the army of Hampton rested nigh unto lake Champlain; and about the same time he moved towards the borders of the king.

And Wilkinson sent a messenger to him and entreated him to come and meet him, and join the two armies together at the village of St. Regis.

The same night Wilkinson with his army crossed the great river St. Lawrence, near by the strong hold of Prescot, which lieth in the dominions of the king.

And he moved down with about six thousand men towards the hold of Montreal, until he came to a place called Crystler's Farms, near unto *Williamsburgh*.

Now at this place, on the eleventh day of the eleventh month, a strong band of the men of war of Britain, from Kingston and round about, fell upon his army in the rear, and annoyed them greatly.

At length, on the same day, a part of the army of Columbia turned about, and fought against them and drove them back; however it was a sore fight.

Wilkinson, the chief captain who went before the host of Columbia, had been sick many days, and was unable to go forth against them himself.

So he sent some of his brave captains, even Boyd, and Swartwout, and Covington; and the engines of destruction were set to work with great noise and fury; and the valiant Covington was wounded unto death.

Moreover, the loss of the men of Columbia that day was an hundred slain, and two hundred two score and ten wounded, and the loss of the king was about an hundred four score and one.

After this battle the army of Wilkinson moved along down the St. Lawrence until they came to *Barnhearts*, near *Cornwall*, where they met the valiant *Brown*.

Now this place lieth on the north side of the river, and on the other side lieth St. Regis, where Wilkinson, the chief captain, expected to be joined by the army of Hampton from Champlain.

But in this he was disappointed; for, lo! Hampton sent one of his captains, whose name was Atkinson, to Wilkinson, with the tidings that he had declined to meet him, and was returning to his camp on the lake.

Now when the army of Wilkinson heard those things, they were discouraged; and all the plans that were well devised by *Armstrong*,[68] the chief captain, and scribe of the great Sanhedrim, were of no avail.

So the army of Wilkinson crossed the river again and came into the land of Columbia, at *French Mills*, near St. Regis; where they went into winter quarters.

And the men of Columbia, even the great Sanhedrim, were disappointed in their expectations.

Moreover, Hampton received much blame in the thing; and he was even taxed with the crime of drinking too freely of the strong waters.

But the imaginary evils which the children of men commit are oftentimes graven in brass, whilst their actual good deeds are written in sand.

---

[68] Gen. Armstrong, Secretary at War.

Neither shall it be forgotten here, that when the shivering soldiers of Columbia were suffering with cold in the north,

The lovely and patriotic daughters Of Columbia, blest with tenderness, remembered them, and sent them coverings for their hands and for their feet,

Even from the fleece: of their fathers' flocks, they wrought them with their own hands, and distributed them with a good heart.

And, for their kindness and humanity, the poor soldier blessed them, and their virtues were extolled by the men of Columbia throughout the land.

CHAP. XXXVII.

Newark burnt—Fort George evacuated—Niagara frontier laid Waste—Buffalo burnt.

In the meantime, however, the strong vessels of Chauncey went out and brought Harrison, and the remnant of his army, from Fort George to Sackett's Harbor, to protect the place.

But they left McClure behind, with the men under him; being for the most part husbandmen, called militia, and volunteers.

And they were eager to be led on to the battle; but the term for which their services were engaged expired, and they returned every man to his own house.

So McClure, the chief captain of the fort, called a council of his officers, and they agreed to depart to the strong hold of Niagara.

And they took their destroying engines and the black dust, and the bread and meat of the army, and carried them across the river.

Likewise they put a lighted match to the black dust, in the fort, and it was rent asunder with a great noise, as it were of thunder and an earthquake.

Moreover, they burnt the town of Newark, before they departed, which happened on the tenth day of the twelfth month.

Howbeit, they gave the inhabitants time to flee before they put the burning torch to their dwellings; nevertheless, it was an evil thing, and pleased not the people of Columbia.

The men of Columbia were not cruel, and they put none of the inhabitants of the town to the sword.

After this, it came to pass on the nineteenth day of the same month, early in the. morning before the dawning of the day, about fifteen hundred of the savages and soldiers of the king crossed the river and went against Niagara.

And they fell upon them unawares, while they were yet asleep in their tents; and overcame them, and took the fort, and put the garrison to the sword; even the women and children suffered under the savage tomahawk.

Now the people of Columbia, who were massacred that day, were about two hundred two score and ten.

But the captain of the hold, whose name was *Leonard*, was charged with the evil; for he had left the fort, and neglected that duty which should ever be the pride of a soldier.

Nevertheless, when they had committed all this horrid slaughter, the barbarians were not fully glutted with murder;

So they went against the little villages of *Lewistown, Manchester, Youngstown*, and *Tuscarora*, and burnt them with fire, and slew the poor and helpless that dwelt round about the place.

After which, at the close of the year, they went against the beautiful village of Buffalo, and burnt it also; and made it a ruin and a desolation.

CHAP. XXXVIII.

Cruise of the U. S. Frigate Essex, D. Porter, commander— her defence and capture, at Valparaiso.

Now while the great lakes and rivers were bound in fetters of ice, and the armies of Columbia slumbered in the winter camps of the north;

And whilst the conquering sword of Jackson spread ruin and desolation among the misguided savages of the south;

Lo! new scenes of warfare appeared upon the waters of the great deep.

In the first year of the war *David*, whose sur-name was *Porter*, sailed from the shores of Columbia towards the south, that he might capture the vessels of the men of Britain.

And the ship which he commanded was one of the strong vessels of Columbia, called the *Essex*.

Now David was a valiant man, and he had contrived a plan to annoy the commerce of Britain in the waters of the great *Pacific Ocean*.

So, in process of time, he passed around the furthermost part of the land of Columbia, which is called *Cape Horn*, and lieth far to the south; near the country of *Patagonia*, which is inhabited by the barbarians, and sailed towards the haven of *Valparaiso*.

From whence, leaving *Chili* to the south, he moved along the coast of *Peru*, till he came to *Lima*, where it never rains:

A country where gold and silver are found in abundance, and where there is one continual summer, and the trees blossom throughout the year.

Again, he prepared his vessels, and sailed from Lima towards the north, until he fell upon the islands of *Gallapagos*; called the enchanted islands.

Now these islands lie upon the west side of the great continent of Columbia, under a meridian sun, beneath the girdle of the world.

Hereabouts he captured a multitude of the merchant ships of Britain, laden with rich merchandize, and silver and gold.

And he fixed a score of the destroying engines into one of the ships he had taken; and made her a fighting vessel, and called her name *Essex Junior*, and a man, whose name was *Downs*, he made captain thereof.

And he fell upon the fishermen of Britain, and captured those who went out to catch the mighty whales, which afford oil to give us light in the night time, and the bones thereof shade our daughters from the scorching sun of the noon-day.

Moreover, David went to an island where there dwelt wild savages, and established himself so that he could go out and return whensoever he chose.

And when he departed from the island, which he called after the chief governor of the land of Columbia in those days,[69] he left some of his men, with the weapons of war, to defend the place.

Now David was a grievous thorn in the side of Britain, and he almost destroyed her commerce in the *South Seas*:

Inasmuch as he put the wise men of the king to their wits end; for they were unable to out-sail him and take him captive.

---

[69] Madison Island.

So they sent their strong ships in search of him, by *two's*, over the whole face of the waters of the *Southern Ocean*; and the expense thereof would have made more than *two feasts for the Prince Regent*, who governed England in the name of his father.

However, it came to pass, that David returned again in his ship to the haven of Valparaiso; and the vessel, called the Essex Junior, accompanied him.

Now Downs, who commanded her, had been to the place before, and conducted the prizes of David there, and brought him the tidings that he was likely to be ensnared upon the waters.

So whilst David was there, on the twenty-eighth day of the third month, in the eighteen hundred and fourteenth year of the Christian era,

He looked around, and behold! he saw two of the strong ships of Britain approaching, for the purpose of hemming him in; the one called the *Phoebe*, and the other the *Cherub*.

But his heart sank not within him, for he knew no cowardice; but, with the wisdom of a brave man, he strove to escape, as the vessels were too powerful for him.

But the winds were adverse, and blew hard, and prevented the tacklings of his ship from taking effect:

Nevertheless, David said unto the captains of the king, Come singly, and not like cowards, upon me; then shall ye receive the thunders of the freemen of Columbia abundantly;

And her liberty shall not suffer, although in the contest ye may destroy my vessel upon the face of the waters.

But *Hillyar*, the captain of the king's ship called the *Phoebe*, was afraid lest he should be overcome.

Now, when David found he was unable to make good his escape, he drew nigh the land, that he might be protected by the great law of nations; for it was a place friendly to both parties.

But in this he was deceived; for the authorities of Spain trembled at the nod of the servants of Britain, in whom there was no faith.

So both vessels came upon him, like ravenous wolves, in the very haven of Valparaiso; thus transgressing the law of nations, and committing an outrage which hath few examples under the sun.

And they set their engines to work upon the Essex with all their might.

Nevertheless, David fought against them with desperation, for there was no hope left for him to escape; neither did he expect mercy.

And he held out for more than the space of two hours, when he became overpowered; having his ship a sinking wreck, covered with blood, and on fire; with about an hundred and fifty of his men slain and maimed.

So after David had fought hard, he became captive to the ships of the king; who had also some of their men slain, and some wounded.

Moreover, Hillyar gave him praise and called him a man of courage; for he fought against two strong ships of Britain.

And David made a covenant with Hillyar, in which the Essex Junior was given unto him and his men, that they might return in her again to their own country.

And it came to pass, in the seventh month of the same year of the battle, David arrived in the city of New-York; having been absent about two years.

Now when the people of Columbia beheld the valiant Porter, they were rejoiced with exceeding great joy; inasmuch as they untackled the horses from before his chariot, and drew him through the city.

And they made a sumptuous feast for him, and invited a multitude of guests; and spent the day in gladness and mirth.

CHAP. XXXIX.

Capture of the u. S. Sloop of War Frolic, the British frigate Orpheus—capture of the British sloop of war L'Epervier, by the Peacock, Capt. Warrington—capture of the Reindeer, by the Wasp, Capt. Blakely—the Avon captured and sunk— U. S. Vessels Syren and rattlesnake captured—Admiral Cochrane declares the whole American coast in a state of blockade.

Now it happened, on the twenty-first day of the fourth month of the eighteen hundred and fourteenth year, that one of the strong ships of the king, called the *Orpheus*;

Being upon the waters of the great deep, fell in with a small vessel of the United States, called the *Frolic*, and made capture thereof.

However, in the same month, not many days afterwards, a fighting vessel of Columbia, called the *Peacock*, commanded by the brave *Warrington*, met one of the vessels of the king.

Now they were about equal in force; and the name of the vessel of Britain was called *L'Epervier*, and the captain's name was *Wales*.

And they sat the engines of destruction to work, and fought with great fury for the space of forty minutes;

When the mariners of Columbia overcame the servants of the king, and the vessel of Britain struck her red-cross to the ship of Warrington.

And there were slain and wounded of the servants of the king about twenty and three; but there were none slain of the people of Columbia.

Moreover, Warrington gat about an hundred and twenty thousand pieces of silver, that were in the vessel.

And he received great praise throughout the land for this gallant exploit.

And the great Sanhedrim thanked him and gave him a medal of gold.

Likewise, the people of *Savannah*, a chief town in the state of *Georgia*, being a thousand miles to the south of New-York, honored him greatly.

For he had brought both vessels into their port; and there were much rejoicings; and a rich feast was prepared for him by the people.

Moreover, it came to pass, on the twenty-eighth day of the sixth month, that one of the fighting ships of Columbia, called the *Wasp*, met a vessel of the king upon the ocean, called the *Reindeer*; after one of the swift running animals of Columbia.

Now the Wasp was commanded by a man of courage; whose name was *Blakeley*.

And a dreadful battle began; and the mischievous weapons of destruction showered around with tremendous noise.

Nevertheless, Blakeley ran down upon the Reindeer, and in about twenty minutes made her a captive unto the ship of Columbia.

But her captain was slain, and she was as it were a wreck upon the waters; so Blakeley destroyed her.

The loss of the king, in killed and wounded that day, was about seventy and five; and five of the children of Columbia were slain, and about a score maimed.

And the friends of the great Sanhedrim were pleased with the valiant acts of Blakeley.

Moreover, on the twenty-seventh day of the eighth month, the Wasp captured another ship of the king, called the *Avon*, and sunk her to the bottom of the briny deep.

And the slain and the wounded of the Avon, was two score and two.

Howbeit, about the same time, the *Syren* and the *Rattlesnake*[70] fell into the hands of the king.

About this time the whole land of Columbia was *ordered* to be hemmed in by *Cochrane*, a servant of the king, and a chief captain of the navy of Britain.

But all their blockades were of no avail; for the men of Columbia escaped and outwitted them.

---

[70] U. S. schooner and brig, about 14 guns each.

CHAP. XL.

Breaking up of the cantonment at French Mills—affair at La Cole mill—Major Appling captures two hundred British seamen —Gen. Brown captures Fort Erie—battle of Chippawa plains.

Now it came to pass, in the second month of the same year in which David gat home to the United States,

That the armies of the north began to be in motion, and departed from the place called *French Mills*, where they were encamped.

And a part thereof moved towards *Plattsburgh*, on lake Champlain; and was commanded by a brave man, whose name was *Macomb*, and Wilkinson, the chief captain, followed after them.

But the other part of the host, commanded by *Jacob*, whose sur-name was *Brown*, went to *Sackett's Harbor*; and from thence against the strong hold of Niagara.

And it was so, that when Wilkinson heard that Jacob had gone against Niagara; he marshalled out his force, and went against a place in the province of the king, called *La-Cole-Mill*, to take it.

Nevertheless, he failed, and lost many men, after which the command of the army was given to a chief captain, whose name was *Izard*,

In the meanwhile many of the evils of warfare were committed on and about the waters of *Ontario* and the great lake *Erie*.

And a gallant captain, whose name was *Appling*,[71] took about two hundred of the mariners of the royal navy of Britain, at a place called *Sandy Creek*, by the waters of lake Ontario: being in the same month that the strong hold of *Oswego* was taken by the men of Britain.

Now on the third day of the seventh month, it came to pass, that Jacob, the chief captain of the host of Columbia, on the borders of the river Niagara,

Having prepared his men beforehand, crossed the river and captured fort Erie, and an hundred thirty and seven of the soldiers of the king, and some of the destroying engines;

And the next day, being the anniversary of the independence of Columbia, after having left some of the men of war to defend the place,

He moved with his host towards the plains of *Chippawa*, where they rested for the night.

On the next day Jacob assembled his captains of fifties, and his captains of hundreds, and spake unto them, saying,

Lo! the army of the king are mighty men of valor, and their numbers are great, even those who have fought under the banners of *Wellington*,[72] the chief warrior of Britain; and *Riall*, the chief captain of the host, is a man of great experience:

Nevertheless, be not disheartened; but let us beware that we be not ensnared.

So he prepared his army to go against the host of Britain, in battle array; and the soldiers of Columbia shouted for the battle.

---

[71] Major Appling.
[72] Lord Wellington,

Now the army of Britain rested upon the plains of Chippawa, and were ready to meet the army of Columbia; they shouted aloud, and inflamed their blood with the strong waters of Jamaica.

And they put fire to the black dust of the destroying engines; and a great noise issued from the mouths thereof.

Moreover, they vomited fire and smoke and brimstone wonderfully, and with the movements of the armies the dust of the earth arose and overshadowed the field of slaughter.

And the heavy balls of iron whistled about them in abundance.

However, the skill of Jacob, and his brave captains, became manifest, and they drove the slaves of Britain before them,

And compelled them to flee to their strong entrenchments at Fort George and Fort Niagara.

And the field of battle was covered with the slain and the maimed; even eight hundred men.

And the slain and wounded of the servants of the king were about five hundred.

So Jacob and his army gat great praise, and all the warriors of Columbia that fought that day;

Amongst whom were the volunteers of the states of *New-York* and *Pennsylvania*, who were led on by the gallant *Porter*.[73]

And *Ripley* was there, and the brave *Scott*, who went out and fought in the heat of the battle.

---

[73] Gens. Porter, Ripley, and Scott.

CHAP. XLI.

Battle of Bridgewater.

Now about this time there was peace among the strong powers of Europe; and the strength of Britain was free to be employed against the people of Columbia.

So she increased her navy on the shores of Columbia, and strengthened her armies in Canada; and sent skilful men to conduct them and to fight her battles:

And, in her spite, she emptied out the vials of her vengeance upon the United States.

Notwithstanding, it came to pass, on the twenty-fifth day of the same month,

That another bloody battle was fought hard by, at a place called *Bridgewater*, from whence ye might behold the stupendous water-falls of Niagara.

There the army of Britain came out against Jacob, with a host of five thousand chosen men.

Now the numbers of the host of Columbia were less than the host of the king, who were commanded by two chief captains, the one named *Drummond*, and the other *Riall*;

Nevertheless, Jacob went out against them and gave them battle: and the army of Columbia shouted aloud; and the battle waxed hot beyond measure.

And it lasted for the space of seven hours; even until the midnight.

The huge engines of destruction roared as the loud thunder, and the blaze thereof was like unto flashes of lightning.

But it came to pass, that the army of Columbia drove the *invincibles* of Wellington from the field.

The valiant *Miller*, with his band, rushed upon the soldiers of the king, with the sharp points of his weapons of war, that faintly glittered in the light of the moon, and overcame them.[74]

Moreover, Drummond, the chief captain of the king, was wounded, and nigh being made captive; and Riall, the chief captain, was taken and fell into the hands of the brave Jessup.[75]

And Jacob, the chief captain of the host of Columbia, was sorely wounded; and the brave Scott was wounded to a certain degree.

However, this was a dreadful battle, fought army against army, and blood and slaughter covered the green fields.

The loss of the king, was about a thousand and two hundred fighting men, who came to the land of Columbia to lose the honor they won in Europe.

The loss of the men of Columbia was also very great; being an hundred three score and ten slain, and more than five hundred maimed.

Now as Jacob, the chief captain of the host of Columbia was wounded, the charge was given to the valiant *Ripley*, and the army returned to the strong hold of Fort Erie.

---

[74] Miller's brilliant charge on the enemy.
[75] Major Jessup, of the 25th Reg.

And Jacob and his brave men gained great praise throughout the land of Columbia.

CHAP. XLII.

Assault on Fort Erie, by the British, under Gen. Drummond—Gen. Brown resumes his command—sallies out of Fort Erie against the British camp—MacArthur's expedition into Canada.

And it came to pass, on the fourth day of the next month, being the same day that the gallant *Morgan*, with two hundred and two score men, drove a thousand soldiers of the king from before *Black Rock*,

A chief captain of Columbia, whose name was *Gaines*,[76] arrived from Sackett's Harbor at Fort George; and took the command thereof.

And it was so, that on the following day the army of the king approached towards the fort, and encamped themselves.

Moreover, they threw up breast-works and prepared their battering-rams, with intent to destroy the place, and make captives of the men of Columbia.

For as the *invincible* soldiers of Britain had lost a *great deal of honor*, they longed to gain *some favor* in the sight of the king, their master; so they sat their bombs and their engines at the work of destruction.

And on the fifteenth day of the month, after they had prepared themselves, they rushed forth with all their might against the strong hold of Columbia.

---

[76] Gen. Gaines.

And as their deeds were evil, they began in the dead of the night, when the howlings of the wild-wolf are heard from afar, and the steady roar of distant water-falls, catches the ear of the drowsy centinel.

Lo! it was a night dark and gloomy; and the very clouds of heaven wept for the folly of man.[77]

Quickly did the weapons of murder disturb and trouble the general silence.

Their thunders roared around the battlements; and the sudden blaze, from the engines, was as a thousand flashes of lightning.

But the men of Columbia were not asleep; for they met them at the onset: thrice the men of Britain came, and thrice were they driven back.

About this time, a man of Columbia, who was sorely wounded, begged of an officer of the king that his life might be spared;

But the captain, whose name was *Drummond*,[78] to whom he spake, refused him quarters; and, taking an oath, he swore and cursed the men of Columbia, saying, Even as I slay thee, so shall it be with ye all.

Thus violating the commandment of God, which sayeth, THOU SHALT DO NO MURDER.

But the hand of the Lord was stretched out against him; for while he was yet speaking, in the wickedness of his heart, he was smitten dead to the earth.

Now, although the men of Britain did some injury to the fort, they were quickly compelled to depart.

And the slain and wounded of the king that night, were about seven hundred, besides two hundred captives.

---

[77] It was a rainy night.
[78] Col. Drummond.

The loss of the United States was about an hundred men.

Now it came to pass, on the seventeenth day of the next month, when Jacob was recovered of his wounds, and had resumed his command, he sallied out of Fort Erie with his men, and went against the camp of the servants of the king.

And by his bravery and skill, and that of the valiant captains under him, he took and destroyed their strong holds, and slew many of them, so that their loss was about a thousand fighting men.

And the slain and wounded of Jacob's army were two hundred ninety and nine.

Now the valiant deeds of Jacob, and his brave men, are they not written in all the books of the chronicles of the land of Columbia of that day?

After this, on the twenty-first day of the same month, Drummond and the host of Britain, being tired of the noise of the destroying engines of the men of Columbia, went away from the place and rested their army at Queenstown.

About this time *Izard*, the chief captain, arrived at Fort Erie, from Plattsburgh, and, as he was the oldest captain, he took the charge of the army of the north.

During these circumstances, it happened that the brave McArthur, who had remained at the strong hold of Detroit, to defend it,

Moved his army towards *Burlington Heights*, and went more than an hundred miles into the province of Canada.

And the men of Columbia that went with him were valiant men from the state of Kentucky and Ohio; in number about eight hundred.

Victory perched upon their arms, and they slew some of the servants of the king, and made many prisoners, and returned again with the loss of one man.

In the meanwhile, the army of Izard crossed the river and returned from Erie to the borders of Columbia, in the latter part of the year, and went into their winter camps at Buffalo.

CHAP. XLIII.

Attack on Stonington, by the British ships of war, which are defeated and driven off.

In these days the strong powers of Britain strove hard to quench the fire of Columbian Liberty.

But it was lighted up by the band of heaven, and not to be extinguished by the insignificant and self-created gods of the earth.

Now it came to pass, on the ninth day of the eighth month of the same year,

That the mighty ships of Britain came and opened their thundering engines upon the little town of *Stonington*, which lieth in the state of *Connecticut*, in the east.

But the inhabitants of the place were bold and valiant men, and they scorned to make a covenant with the servants of the king.

Although *Hardy*,[79] the chief captain of the king's ships, had threatened to destroy the place; saying, Remove from the town your women and your children, who are innocent and fight not.

Thus showing more righteousness than any of the king's captains; albeit, he gave them only the space of one hour to depart.

---

[79] Com. Hardy, a captain under Lord Nelson, at the battle of Trafalgar.

So the men of Columbia let the destroying engines loose upon the vessels, and shot the *yankee-balls* amongst them plentifully, and compelled them to depart:

Notwithstanding, they had but two of the destroying engines in the place.

However, on the eleventh day of the same month, they were again forced to put them in motion.

For, in the mean time, Hardy had sent a messenger to the inhabitants, saying,

If ye will not prove wicked, and will refrain from sending your evil *torpedoes* amongst our vessels, then will we spare your town.

Now Hardy was mightily afraid of these torpedoes, (the history whereof is written in the fiftieth book of these chronicles) and he trembled at the sound of the name thereof.

Nevertheless, the people of Stonington refused his request.

So the ships of Britain came again and they brought another strong ship of the king to help them to take the place.

But once more the valiant sons of Connecticut made them fly for safety: and they came not again.

And the gallant conduct of the people of Stonington gained them much praise, even from the great Sanhedrim of the people.

Thus would the children of Columbia have done, in many other places, but for the false words and wickedness of traitorous men.

CHAP. XLIV.

Affairs in the Chesapeake—British army move up the Patuxent—land and march towards the city of Washington—prepare themselves for battle at Bladensburgh.

Now the mighty fleet of Britain, that troubled the waters of the great Bay of Chesapeake, commanded by Cockburn the wicked, continued their depredations.

The number of their fighting ships were increased, and the soldiers of the king had come thither in multitudes from the island of Britain.

For the war which she had waged against the mighty ruler of *France*,[80] was at an end; and all their men of war were idle; so they sent them against the men of Columbia, who slew them with terrible slaughter.

Now the numbers of the servants and soldiers of the king, in and about the Chesapeake, were little fewer than ten thousand.

And they moved up the great river, which is called the *Potowmac*, and the river *Patuxent*, which lieth to the east thereof.

So, as they passed along, they did much damage; and destroyed abundance of the sweet-scented plant of Virginia, burning it with fire.

Now this weed is a native of the land of Columbia, and groweth not on the island of Britain:

---

[80] Buonaparte.

Therefore, the nostrils of the slaves of Britain were regaled with the scent thereof, for the king had put a silver bar[81] against its plentiful use, throughout his whole dominions.

However, it came to pass, about the twentieth day of the same month, that the whole army of Britain gat out of their vessels and their boats, at a place called *Benedict*, being towards the head of the river Patuxent.

And a man of great experience in matters of warfare, surnamed *Ross*, was chief captain of the host of Britain.

So they marched on towards *Washington*, which lieth on the waters of the Potowmac, and is called the chief city of the land of Columbia; where the great Sanhedrim assemble themselves together.

And they journied on until they came to a place called *Bladensburgh*, which lieth to the east of the city, not far off.

And Cockburn staid not behind, for his heart thirsted after blood and murder.

Now this was on the twenty-fourth day of the eighth month, in the one thousand eight hundred and fourteenth year of the Christian era.

And the army of Columbia that went out to meet the host of Britain, was commanded by a brave man, whose name was *Winder*.

But it was in the heat of summer, and the husbandmen of Columbia, that went out to defend the place, were weary, for they had travelled many miles from the house of their fathers.

Moreover, their numbers were few at the onset; for those that were journeying on their way came not in time.

---

[81] Tax on tobacco, manufactured in England, is very heavy.

Nevertheless, they who came prepared themselves for the fight, in the hope that they might not be overcome by the servants of the king*

And it was so, that when Ross, the chief captain of the host of Britain, drew nigh the place, and saw that the men of Columbia were bent on giving him hindrance,

He addressed the officers and the men of his army, and encouraged them, saying,

Lo! we are stronger than the host of Columbia; therefore, let us go with all our might against their chief city, and make capture thereof,

And burn it with fire, and take their chief governor, and bind him hand and foot, and bring him before the king.

Moreover, let us surround the temple of the great Sanhedrim of the nation, and endeavor to catch them, even as the huntsman catcheth *foxes*.

Then shall we strike terror throughout the land of Columbia, and the arms of the king, our master, shall be encircled with glory.

The spirit of the people will be broken; they will bow down to the servants of the king: and all the nations will behold the *valiant deeds of Britain*.

CHAP. XLV.

Capture of Washington—sacking of Alexandria—death of Sir Peter Parker.

Now, when Ross, the chief captain, had done speaking, they sent forth their fire-brands, and sat their destroying engines to work, and cast balls of destruction and death.

Nevertheless, the men of Columbia were not dismayed, but poured out their thunders upon them in abundance.

And *Joshua*, sur-named *Barney*, who commanded the vessels of Columbia nigh the place, with his brave men, went out upon the land, and fought against them with desperation.

For he had ordered his little fleet to be burnt with fire, that the men of Britain might not profit thereby, and it blew up in the air with a loud noise.

Now Joshua was in the heat of the battle; and his destroying engines slew the men of Britain on all sides: however, he was wounded and made captive.

But the servants of the king treated Joshua well, and honored him for his bravery.

Now James, the chief governor, and the counsellors, and the scribes of the great Sanhedrim, went out to see the battle, and to contrive for the safety of the city.

And Monroe,[82] the chief scribe of the great Sanhedrim, was there; and Armstrong,[83] and many other friends of the land of Columbia.

Nevertheless, the wisdom of all their plans failed them; and they were sorely grieved to behold the husbandmen and the army of Winder, the chief captain, flee before the host of Britain.

But they were misled in their calculations; and they were now unable to prevent the evil.

Neither did the men of war they counted upon arrive in time to catch the army of the king.

Therefore, the host of Columbia fled, and went beyond the city, and passing through *Georgetown*, rested at a place called *Montgomery Court-house*.

And the slain and maimed of the king, were about four hundred: those of the men of Columbia about two score.

Now it was about the going down of the sun, when the host of the king polluted the Citadel of Freedom, and with their unhallowed footsteps violated the Temple of Liberty.

And Cockburn and Ross led the savage band of Britain into the midst of the city.

And the men of Columbia gnashed their teeth, and bit their lips with vexation; for the thing might have been prevented.[84]

---

[82] Hon. James Monroe, Sec'ry of State.

[83] Gen. Armstrong.

[84] Whatever may be individual sentiment, it has been, and still is the general opinion of the best informed, that there was sufficient time to have had the place entrenched and fortified, if necessary, with an hundred pieces of cannon; and at least to have kept the enemy at bay until a sufficient force were assembled to have cut off his retreat. But to expect raw militia to meet and repulse, in an open plain, solid columns of regular troops, superior in numbers as well as discipline, must be preposterous. Who is to blame in the business we

Nevertheless, it proved a blessing, for it united the people of Columbia as one man, against the tyrants of the earth.

Now the place that had been pitched upon to build the chief city, was in a fine country, and a beautiful spot, in the *District of Columbia*.

But the inhabitants round about the *City of Washington* were few; for they had, as it were, just begun to build it.

There was much ground laid out for the city, even six thousand four hundred square furlongs; but the buildings therein were not many; neither was it fortified.

So when the servants of the king came to the place, they looked around, in surprise, and cried out with astonishment, saying,

Lo! the city hath fled with the people, for there are but an handful of houses in the place.

However, the next day they began the work of destruction, like unto the barbarians of ancient times; for their wickedness followed after them as the shadow followeth after the substance.

And they destroyed the beautiful edifices with fire, even the palace of the great Sanhedrim.

Now Cockburn hated that his wicked deeds should be handed down to future generations, so he went and destroyed, with his own hands, the chief *printing-office* [85] of the city, and scattered the *types* abroad.

---

presume not to say but hope the evil may be remedied against a future day. Had the same energy and industry been exercised there, that were displayed by the patriotic citizens of New-York, in erecting fortifications for the defence of their capital, we might have been spared the mortification that followed the capture of the seat of government.

[85] Office of the National Intelligencer.

Thus did he, even Cockburn, like an ignorant savage, stamp his own name with infamy, and make it to become a reproach amongst all mankind.

Science and learning blushed at the champions of England, who had been represented as the bulwark of religion; but who were, in reality, the supporters of idolatry; the staff of *Juggernaut*, the false god of India.

Now the *art of printing* was not known among the ancients; for it was invented in these latter days, even in the fourteen hundred and fortieth year of the Christian era.

It was the helpmate of Freedom, and when the light which it spread burst forth upon the world, it began to open the eyes of man, and to destroy the poisonous weeds that choaked the growth of Liberty.

Moreover, to complete the vandalism of Cockburn and Ross, they fell upon the printed books of the great Sanhedrim.

Even those that had been gathered together for instruction; the toil of many years, containing the learning and wisdom of ages.

And they consumed them with fire; thus striving to turn man back to the ages of ignorance and darkness.

Now, THOMAS, whose sur-name was JEFFERSON, who had been a scribe in the days of Washington, and a chief governor of the land of Columbia, in times past; a man whom the people esteemed for his virtue,

When he heard of their wickedness; how, savage-like, they had burnt the books which had been written by the wise men of the earth, and preserved from the beginning to that day;

In the goodness of his heart, he wrote unto the great Sanhedrim, when they were assembled together, saying:

Since, like the barbarians of old, whose ignorance might plead for them, the servants of the kingdom of Great Britain have laid waste your chief city, and made it a desolation,

And have trampled upon science, mutilated the monuments of art and industry, destroyed the archives of your nation, and burnt your books with fire;

For your benefit, and for the benefit of my country, I will give unto you my whole Library, which I have selected with care, from my youth upwards, and whatever in your judgment shall be the value thereof, that will I accept.[86]

I am well stricken in years, and must shortly sleep with my fathers; but the last wish of my heart shall be the welfare of my country.

Now Thomas was a philosopher, and a man of great learning, and he had abundance of books of all nations, and in all languages, even ten thousand volumes.

So the great Sanhedrim accepted the offer of Thomas, and they retain the books to this day.

Now it came to pass, in the evening of the same day, on which the vandals of Britain set fire to the city, that the army of the king fled from the place; for the air of Liberty was poison to the followers of tyrants.

Moreover, they left some of their slain and wounded behind, for they were afraid of being caught in a snare by the husbandmen of Columbia.

So they went down to the river and gat into their vessels from whence they came.

---

[86] Mr. Jefferson left it to Congress to make him what compensation they thought proper for his Library.

In the meantime, the inhabitants of *Alexandria*, a town which lieth to the south of the chief city, on the river Potomac, in the state of Virginia,

Being smitten with fear, sent to Cockburn and Ross, entreating mercy, that they might be spared, if, peradventure, they made a covenant in good faith with them, and surrendered themselves.

And the chief captains of Britain agreed to the capitulation of the town, and to vouchsafe it protection.

But the people suffered for their foolish confidence; and no one pitied them; for it was of their own seeking.

So it happened, after they had trusted to the faith of the servants of the king; *Gordon*, a captain of the ships in the river Potomac, came up against them before the town;

And took their merchant ships; and compelled the people to open their storehouses, and put into the vessels their flour, even sixteen thousand barrels, and their wine, and their cotton, and a thousand hogsheads of the sweet-scented plant.

So the robbers of the king took them away, sacked the town, and laughed at the people thereof, for trusting to the faith of. British honor.

However, as they passed along down the river, with their ill-gotten treasure, lo! the ships of Britain were assailed, and nigh being destroyed:

For *Rogers*, and *Perry*, and *Porter*, three valiant captains of the navy of Columbia, gave them hindrance and annoyed them greatly.

Perry and Porter raised fortifications upon the borders of the river, and put therein the destroying engines, which, when the vessels came nigh by, they let loose upon them abundantly, and wounded them in their tackling, and slew numbers of their men.

Moreover, the balls which the engines vomited forth, were red and hot from the mouth of the fiery furnace.

Meanwhile, Rogers sent his fire-ships among them to destroy them as they fled; nevertheless they escaped.

Now about this time, being the thirtieth day of the same month, *Peter*, whose surname was *Parker*, who commanded a strong ship of the king, was committing many depredations along the shores of the Chesapeake;

So Peter essayed to go in the nighttime against some husbandmen of Columbia, commanded by the gallant *Reid*,[87] about the borders of the state of *Maryland*;

And when he had landed his men of war, he went out after the husbandmen, and the plunder; but they were upon the watch, and fell upon him, and killed and maimed about two score, and was nigh making captives of them all; and Peter was amongst the slain.

Now when the news of the taking of the chief city of Columbia, and the sacking of Alexandria was received in Britain, at first the people rejoiced, saying, Now, forsooth, have we conquered these cunning Yankees!

But afterwards they became, for once, ashamed, and hid their faces; for they had heard the judgment of the surrounding nations, by whom their vandalism was condemned.

---

[87] Col. Reid.

CHAP. XLVI.

British, under Gov. Prevost, go against Plattsburgh—Com. Macdonough captures the British squadron on Lake Champlain.

Nevertheless, if difficulties and disasters befel the people of Columbia in the south, lo! there was a wreath of laurels weaving for them in the north.

Behold! a mighty army of the king had assembled together at the village of Champlain, between *Plattsburg* and *Montreal*; nigh unto the place where *Forsyth* the warrior, the second *Sumter*,[88] was slain:

For the Prince Regent had commanded his servants to go forth into the heart of the land of Columbia, and separate the states of the east from the rest of the country.

So it came to pass, about the fifth day of the ninth month, that the host of Britain appeared before the village of Plattsburgh; which lieth about three hundred miles from New-York towards the north.

Now *Prevost*, the governor of Canada, was the commander of the army; and the number of his men of war was about fifteen thousand.

And they began to prepare their battering rams, their bombs and their rockets, and all kinds of instruments of destruction; and they entrenched themselves round about.

Now the strong hold of Plattsburgh was hard by; and the brave *Macomb* was the chief captain of the hold; and the number of his men was about fifteen hundred; being in the proportion of *one* Yankee to *ten* Invincibles.

---

[88] Sumter, a brave officer in the American Revolution.

Howsoever, the valiant husbandmen of the states of *Vermont* and *New-York*, called militia, commanded by *Mooers*, a man of great courage, assembled together, to assist in the defence of the place, on the borders of the river *Saranac*, which emptieth its waters into lake Champlain.

In the meantime, *Downie*, the chief captain of the fleet of Britain upon the lake, had prepared himself to assist Prevost on a certain day appointed.

When he was to come out against the fleet of Columbia, which was commanded by the gallant *Macdonough*.

Accordingly, it came to pass, on the appointed day, being the eleventh of the ninth month, in the one thousand eight hundred and fourteenth year of the Christian era,

And three hundred and sixty-five days after *Oliver* had captured the king's fleet on the waters of Erie,

That the strong vessels of Britain appeared, with their sails spread, moving upon the bosom of lake Champlain, coining against the fleet of Columbia.

Now it was in the morning, about the ninth hour, when Macdonough beheld the fleet of Britain sailing boldly towards him.

And it was so, that the vessels of Columbia were safely moored in the bay of Plattsburgh, where they waited the approach of the enemy; who were the strongest in numbers and in their engines of death.

However, when they were about a furlong off, they cast their anchors, and set themselves in battle array; squadron against squadron.

Now the sound of the battle-drum was heard along the lake, and the brave mariners shouted aloud for the fight.

Then began their destroying engines to utter their voices, and it was like unto the voice of mighty thunders.

And the same hour, the armies on the shore began the dreadful battle with their roaring engines.

So that on the land and on the waters the fire and smoke were abundant, and the noise thereof was tremendous beyond measure.

And the battle waxed hot, and the vessels of Downie fought bravely against the vessels of Macdonough:

Nevertheless, the Lord of hosts favored the men of Columbia, and they overcame the servants of the king.

For in about the space of three hours, the valiant Macdonough and his brave men, made capture of the whole fleet of Britain, save a few gun-boats, that made good their escape.

Now the killed and wounded of the king's fleet, were an hundred ninety and four; and Downie, the chief captain, was among the slain.

Moreover, the number of the captives of the men of Britain was about four hundred.

Now Macdonough was a good man, neither was he full of boasting and vain-glory: he arrogated to himself no praise on account of his success, but ascribed the victory to the pleasure of the Almighty.

And as it is written, in the word of the Lord, DO UNTO ALL MEN AS YE WOULD THEY SHOULD DO UNTO YOU, so he took care of the prisoners, and employed skilful physicians to bind up the wounds of the maimed.

Now were the children of Columbia exceedingly rejoiced; yea, their hearts were made glad; and they praised Macdonough for his noble deeds.

Moreover, the great Sanhedrim honored him; and a piece of land, which over-looketh the lake, was given unto him, for an inheritance;

That, in his old age, and when he was well stricken in years, he might behold with joy the strength of his youth; and smile upon the spot where, fleet to fleet, he triumphed over the enemies of freedom.

And where his children's children might point, and say, It was there the guardian angel of Columbia permitted our father to humble the pride of Britain.

CHAP. XLVII.

Battle of Plattsburgh—defeat Of Sir George Prevost.

Now while Macdonough was capturing the royal fleet of Britain, upon the lake, the gallant *Macomb* scattered destruction amidst the army of *Prevost*.

And the battle raged with great violence, and the men of Britain strove hard to pass over the river called *Saranac*;

But the men of war of Columbia, who were upon the opposite side of the water, opposed them, and slew them with great slaughter.

And the brave *Grosvenor*, and *Hamilton*, and *Riley*, and the gallant *Cronk*, drove them back from crossing the bridges.

Likewise, many were slain in the river, so that the waters of the Saranac were dyed with the blood of the servants of the king.

But Macomb kept the engines at work, and *Brooks*, and *Richards*, and *Smith*, who were in the forts, displayed much valor, and caused the engines to vomit fire and smoke, and balls of heavy metal.

Howsoever, when Prevost saw that the king's fleet was captured, he began to be disheartened, and his whole army was amazed.

Notwithstanding this, they continued to cast their balls, and their rockets, and their bomb-shells, and their *sharpnells*, with all their might.

Now these sharpnells were unknown even to the children of Columbia, for they were lately invented by the wise men of Britain.

However, the people of Columbia trusted in the strength of their *arms*, more than in the strength of these *shells*, so they used them not.

Nevertheless, the army of the king fought hard with their battering-rams against the strong hold of Columbia, until the setting of the sun, when their noises were silenced by the brave band of Columbia.

So the same night, Prevost, and the invincibles of the king, fled towards the strong bold of *Montreal*; leaving their sick and wounded behind to the mercy of the men of Columbia; destroying their provisions, which in their haste they could not carry away.

And the men of Columbia followed them a little way, and slew some and made many captives.

Thus were the men of war of Britain conquered in the north, army against army, fleet against fleet, and squadron against squadron.

And the killed and wounded of the army of the king that day, were about a thousand men; and about three hundred, who were tired of their bondage, left the service of the king,[89] and joined the banners of the great Sanhedrim.

Now Macomb received much praise for his bravery; and his name shall be remembered by ages yet unborn.

Moreover, he spake well of all the officers and men who fought with him.

And Mooers, who commanded the brave husbandmen of New-York and Vermont, and *Strong*, the valiant chief captain of the men called volunteers, had great honor for their noble deeds.

Likewise, *Appling*, and *Wool*, and *Leonard*, and *Sproul*, distinguished themselves among the brave.

---

[89] Deserters.

But when the news of the capture of the fleet, and the defeat of their mighty army, reached the lords of Britain, they put their fingers in their ears, that they might not hear it:

Neither would they believe it; but when they found it was so of a truth, they were enraged out of measure.

And their wise men and their counsellors said, Lo! we have only been trifling with these Yankees; now let us send forth a mighty fleet and an army to overwhelm them.

CHAP. XLVIII.

Attack on Baltimore, by the British army, under Gen. Ross, and the fleet under Admirals Cochrane and Cockburn.

Now when Ross and Cockburn returned from their burning and pillaging, and all the barbarities they committed at Washington, the chief city, and the neighborhood thereof;

Emboldened by the success of their unrighteous deeds, they gathered together their army and their navy, and essayed to go against the city of *Baltimore*, which lieth in the state of *Maryland*;

That they might commit the like wickedness, in which they had taken so much pleasure at Hampton, Havre-de-Grace, and Washington.

But they had a mightier place than Washington to go against; for Baltimore is a great city, containing therein about fifty thousand souls, and the people had entrenched it round about, and made it a strong place.

So it came to pass, the next day after Macdonough had captured the fleet of Britain, on lake Champlain, being the twelfth day of the ninth month,

That their vessels and transports came to a place called *North Point*, which lieth at the entrance of the river *Petapsco*, about an hundred furlongs from the city, and began to put their men of war upon the shore.

And the. number of their chosen fighting men, who were landed, were about eight thousand.

And when they were all moved out of the boats, Ross, the chief captain, conducted them on towards the city.

As they moved along their instruments of war glittered in the beams of the sun; and the waving of their squadrons was like the troubled waters of the ocean.

However, when they came to a place called *Bear Creek*, lo! the army of Columbia met them in battle array.

For, when the gallant young men of Baltimore heard the rumor, that the slaves of Britain were coming upon them;

With the spirit of freemen, they grasped their weapons of war in their hands, and went out to meet them without fear; resolved to conquer or to die.[90]

For well they knew, that life would be a burthen to them, when their habitations were consumed with fire; their parents slaughtered; and the innocence of their wives and their sisters violated.

Now the name of the chief captain of the army of Columbia was *Samuel*, whose surname was *Smith*:[91] a valiant man, who had fought in the days of Washington, and gained much honor.

Moreover, Samuel was a man well-stricken in years, and he had many brave captains under him; even *Stricker*, and *Stansbury*, and *Winder* were with him.

Now it was somewhat after the midday when the engines of destruction began their roaring noises:

And the fire and smoke were vomited forth out of their mouths, so that the light of the sun was hidden by the means of the black clouds that filled the air.

---

[90] Although it may be said the British were not conquered; yet they were defeated.
[91] Gen. Smith.

And their rockets, and all their instruments of death, which the sons of men have employed their understandings to invent, were used abundantly.

Now the battle waxed hot, and the gallant Stricker, and his brave men, fought hard; and it was a dreadful fight,

Inasmuch as the slain and wounded of the king that day, were about four hundred; and the loss of the men of Columbia was two hundred.

Moreover, Ross, the chief captain of the host of Britain, was amongst the slain; a boy, who had accompanied his father to battle, had taken dreadful aim at Ross, with his rifle, and killed him; and the people of Columbia grieved only because it was not Cockburn the wicked, who had fallen; for a man, whose name was *O'Boyle*, had offered five hundred pieces of silver for each of his ears.

Nevertheless, the men of Columbia were not powerful enough to overcome the servants of the king; so they drew back into their entrenchments, and strong holds; that were upon the high places round about the city.

And *Rogers*, and *Findley*, and *Harris*, and *Stiles* were among the captains of the strong holds; and were all faithful men.

But it came to pass, the next day, when the men of Britain saw that the children of Columbia were well prepared for battle, that they were afraid to go against the strong holds.

So in the middle of the night, which was dark and rainy, they departed from the place, and returned to their vessels, that they might escape the evil that was preparing for them.

Moreover, they took the dead body of Ross, their chief captain, with them, and cast it into a vessel, filled with the strong waters of Jamaica;

That the instrument of their wickedness might be preserved, and conveyed to the king, their master, and be buried in his own country; for which honor the people envied them not.

Now it came to pass, in the meantime, that Cochrane, and Cockburn the wicked, the chief captains of the mariners of the king, sailed up the river Petapsco, towards the strong hold of *Fort McHenry*, to assail it.

Now the strong hold of McHenry lieth about fifteen furlongs from the city; and the name of the chief captain thereof was *Armistead*, a man of courage.

And when the strong vessels of the king drew nigh unto the fort, they cast their rockets and their bomb-shells into it plentifully, and strove hard to drive the men of Columbia away.

But the gallant Armistead let the destroying engines loose upon them, without mercy; and they cast out their thunders, winged with death, among the servants of the king.

The loud groans of their wounded floated upon the waters, with an awful horror that shocked the ear of humanity.

And it was so, that when Cockburn found he could not prevail against the strong hold, he also departed from the river, neither came they against the place any more.

Now when the men of Columbia heard that Ross, the chief captain of the king, was slain, and the host of Britain was compelled to flee from before the city, they were exceedingly rejoiced.

And the brave defenders of Baltimore had great praise and honor given them throughout the land.

And the names of those who fell in the contest, are they not written on the monument which the gratitude of the people of Baltimore erected to the memory of its defenders?

CHAP. XLIX.

Destruction of the privateer gen. Armstrong, Samuel C. Reid, Captain—Scorpion and Tigress captured— U. S. frigate Adams burnt —Castine—Fort Boyer attacked—destruction of the pirates at Barrataria, by Com. Patterson—Gen. Jackson captures Pensacola, and returns to New-Orleans.

Now the loud and frightful noise of war sounded upon the bosom of the great deep; and the shores of Columbia knew no peace.

The dreadful clangor of arms rung upon the land, and echoed from the mountains; and the groans of suffering victims floated in the air of heaven.

But the Lord favored the people of Columbia, and their armies and their navy gained strength, and prosperity was showered upon them: the voice of war became familiar to those who were strangers to it in times past.

Now on the twenty-sixth day of the ninth month, being in the thirty and ninth year of Columbian Independence,

It came to pass, that a certain private armed vessel of the people of Columbia, called the *General Armstrong*, commanded by *Samuel*, whose surname was *Reid*,

Had cast her anchors in the haven of *Fayal*, an island in the sea, which lieth towards the rising sun, about two thousand miles from the land of Columbia;

A place where, two score and ten years ago, there was a mighty earthquake; and where poisonous reptiles never dwell.

And it was about the dusk of the evening when Samuel saw a number of the strong vessels of Britain hemming him in: so he drew nigh to the shore for safety, for the place was friendly to both powers.

Nevertheless, the boats from the vessels of the king went against Samuel to take his vessel; but with his weapons of war he drove them off and slew numbers of them, so that they were glad to return to their strong ships,

However, they quickly returned with a greater number of boats, and about four hundred men; and Samuel saw them, and prepared to meet them.

The silver beams of the moon danced upon the gently rolling waves of the mighty deep, and the sound of the oar again broke the sweet silence of night.

But, when they came nigh the vessel of Samuel, the men of Columbia poured out destruction upon them with a plentiful hand;

Inasmuch as they were again compelled to depart to their strong vessels, with dreadful loss.

However, about the dawning of the day, one of the strong vessels, called the *Carnation*, came against the vessel of Columbia, and let her destroying engines loose with great fury.

Now *Lloyd*, who commanded the *Plantagenet*, was the chief captain of the squadron of the king, in the place; and he violated the law of nations.

So when Samuel saw that the whole fleet of Britain were bent on destroying his vessel, in defiance of the plighted honor of nations, he ordered her to be sunk.

After which he and his brave mariners ted her, and went upon the shore; and the servants of the king came and burnt her with fire in the neutral port of Fayal.

Nevertheless, they received the reward of their unrighteousness, for much damage was done to their vessels, and their slain and wounded were two hundred two score and ten.

Of the people of Columbia two only were slain and seven maimed!!

And the valiant deeds of Samuel gained him a name amongst the brave men of Columbia.

Now, in the same month, the *Scorpion* and the *Tigress*, two fighting vessels of Columbia, on lake *Huron*, were captured by the men of Britain.

Likewise, about this time, there were numerous other evils that befel the sons of Columbia;

Inasmuch as a brave captain, whose sur-name was *Morris*, was obliged to consume his ship with fire, lest she should fall into the hands of the enemy; and she was called the *Adams*.[92]

Now this was at a place called *Castine*, which was forcibly occupied by the strong ships of Britain, and lieth to the east, in the District of *Maine*: moreover, it became a watering place for the servants of the king.

But when James, the chief governor, and the great Sanhedrim, knew thereof, they sent word to the governor, and offered him soldiers to drive them from the borders of Columbia;

But, lo! the governor, even Caleb the shittamite, refused his aid, for he was afraid of the wrath of the king of Britain.[93]

(Now Caleb, in the hebrew tongue, signifieth a dog; but, verily, this dog was faithless.)

---

[92] U. S. frigate Adams.
[93] See the letter of Sec. Monroe, and Strong's answer.

Moreover, it came to pass, about the same time, that the strong hold of *Fort Boyer*, being at a place called *Mobile-point*, was attacked by the strong ships of Britain.

Now Mobile had lately been the head quarters and the resting-place of the army of Jackson the brave;

But the enemies of Columbia had become tumultuous at a place called, by the Spaniards, *Pensacola*, whither he had departed to quell them;

So that the fort was defended by only a handful of men, commanded by the gallant *Lawrence*.

And the names of the vessels of the king, that assailed the fort, were the *Hermes*, the *Charon*, and the *Sophie*, besides other fighting vessels; which opened their fires upon the strong hold.

Nevertheless, Lawrence was not dismayed, although Woodbine,[94] the white savage, came in his rear, with one of the destroying engines and a howitzer, an instrument of Satan, and about two hundred savages.

So when Lawrence let his engines of death loose upon them, and had showered the whizzing balls amongst them for about the space of three hours, they fled.

And the slaughter on board the ships was dreadful; and about three hundred of the men of Britain were slain, and the Hermes was blown out of the water into the air with an awful noise.

The loss of the people of Columbia that day, was four slain and five maimed.

---

[94] The celebrated Capt. Woodbine, of the British navy.

About this time a band of sea-robbers and pirates, who had established themselves upon the island of *Barrataria*, were committing great wickedness and depredations; and were ready to assist the men of Britain.

But a valiant man, called *Daniel*, sur-named *Patterson*, went against them with his small fighting vessels,[95] and scattered them abroad, and took their vessels, and destroyed their *petty* establishment of sea-robbery.

Now it came to pass, when Jackson heard that Pensacola, the capital of *West-Florida*, had become a resting-place for the enemies of Columbia; and that the men of Britain occupied the place, and had built them a strong hold therein;

From whence they sent forth the weapons of war and the black dust among the savages, to destroy the people of Columbia; and that the servants of the king of Spain were afraid to prevent the wickedness thereof;

Behold! he, even Jackson, went out against the place with a band of five thousand fighting men, the brave sons of Tennessee and other parts of Columbia.

And it was early in the morning of the seventh day of the eleventh month when the host of Columbia appeared before the walls of Pensacola.

And immediately Jackson sat the engines of destruction to work; and the smoke thereof obscured the weapons of war.

Now when the governor of the place heard the noise of the engines of death and the clashing of arms, he was smitten with fear;

Insomuch that Jackson, the chief captain, who with his army had encompassed the place, quickly compelled him to surrender the town, and beg for mercy; which was granted unto him and his people, even the Spaniards.

---

[95] Gun-boats.

Now when the men of Britain saw this, they put the match to the black dust in their strong hold, and it rent the air with tremendous noise.

After which they fled from the land into their strong ships, that were in the haven of Pensacola.

And Jackson, having accomplished his wishes, by intimidating the tools of British villany and murder, returned with his army in triumph to the city of New-Orleans, on the second day of the twelfth month.

CHAP. L.

Steam-boats—Fulton—torpedoes—attempt to blow up the Plantagenet—kidnapping Joshua Penny.

Now it happened that, in the land of Columbia, there arose up wise and learned men, whose cunning had contrived and invented many useful things.

Among these there appeared one whose ingenuity was exceedingly great, inasmuch as it astonished all the inhabitants of the earth:

Now the name of this man was *Robert,* sur-named *Fulton*; (but the cold hand of death fell upon him, and he slept with his fathers, on the twenty and third day of the second month of the eighteen hundred and fifteenth year of the Christian era.)

However, the things which he brought into practice in his life time will be recorded, and his name spoken of by generations yet unborn.

Although, like other men of genius, in these days, he was spoken of but slightly at first; for the people said, Lo! the man is beside himself! and they laughed at him; nevertheless, he exceeded their expectations.

For it came to pass, that (assisted by *Livingston,* a man of wealth, and a lover of arts and learning) he was enabled to construct certain curious vessels, called in the vernacular tongue, *steam-boats.*

Now these steam-boats were cunningly contrived, and had abundance of curious workmanship therein, such as surpassed the comprehension of all the wise men of the east, from the beginning to this day;

Howbeit, they were fashioned somewhat like unto the first vessel that floated upon the waters, which was the ark of Noah, the ninth descendant from Adam;

And, that they might heat the water which produced the steam, there was a fiery furnace placed in the midst of the vessels, and the smoke issued from the tops thereof.

Moreover, they had, as it were, wheels within wheels; and they moved fast upon the waters, even against the wind and the tide.

And they first began to move upon the great river *Hudson*, passing to and fro, from New-York to Albany, in the north, conveying the people hither and thither in safety.

But when the scoffers, the enemies of Fulton, and the gainsayers, saw that the boats moved pleasantly upon the river, they began to be ashamed of their own ignorance and stupidity, and were fain to get into the boats themselves; after which, instead of laughing, they gaped at the inventor with astonishment.

And it came to pass, that the great Sanhedrim were pleased with the thing, inasmuch as they directed a fighting vessel of Columbia to be built after this manner.

So a vessel was built, to carry the destroying engines, even a steam-frigate, and they called her name *Fulton the First*:

And the length thereof was about an hundred cubits, and the breadth thereof thirty cubits:

Moreover, as they had no gophar-wood, they built the vessel partly of the locust-tree, and partly of the majestic oak that flourishes in the extensive forests of Columbia.

But it came to pass, when the wise men and the people of Britain heard of this steam-frigate, they were seized with astonishment and fright; inasmuch as it became a monster in their imaginations.

And they spake concerning it, saying, Lo! the length of this wonder of the world, which hath been invented by these cunning Yankees, is about two hundred cubits, and the breadth thereof an hundred thirty and five cubits:

The number of her destroying engines are very great; and the weight of a ball which she vomiteth forth, is about a thousand five hundred two score and ten shekels:

Moreover, said they, she is prepared to cast forth scalding water in showers upon the servants of the king, which will deform their countenances and spoil their beauty:

Likewise, they have prepared her with two-edged swords, which, by means of the steam of the vessel, issue like lightning out of her sides.

And now, also, the cunning and witchcraft of these Yankees, these sons of Belial, these children of Beelzebub, have invented another instrument of destruction, more subtle than all the rest

Yea, these are mighty evil things, and they are called *torpedoes*, which may be said to signify sleeping devils; which come, as a thief in the night, to destroy the servants of the king; and were contrived by that arch fiend whose name was *Fulton*.

Now these wonderful torpedoes were made partly of brass and partly of iron, and were cunningly contrived with curious works, like unto a clock; and as it were a large ball.

And, after they were prepared, and a great quantity of the black dust put therein, they were let down into the water, nigh unto the strong ships, with intent to destroy them.

And it was so, that when they struck against the bottom of the ship, the black dust in the torpedo would catch fire, and burst forth with tremendous roar, casting the vessel out of the waters and bursting her in twain.

Now these torpedoes were brought into practice during the war, although the war ceased before they did that destruction to the enemies of Columbia, for which they were intended.

However, a certain man of courage and enterprize, whose name was *Mix*, prepared one of the torpedoes, and put it into the waters of the great deep, at a place called *Lyn-Haven Bay*, at the mouth of the great bay of Chesapeake, nigh unto the town of *Norfolk*, in the state of Virginia;

And it moved towards a strong ship of Britain, called the *Plantagenet*, after one of the former princes of England; but an accident happened a little before it reached the vessel, and it burst asunder in the waters with a tremendous noise;

And spouted the water up into the air, as doth the mighty whale, and the sound thereof was, as it were, the voice of thunder,

And the servants of the king were frightened horribly by the means thereof; after which they trembled at the name of torpedo!—and were obliged to guard their vessels in the night, and put a double watch upon them;

Moreover, they condemned this mode of warfare, saying: Verily, this is a foul fashion of fighting; inasmuch as by your cunning ye Yankees take the advantage of us; and the thing is new unto us.

But they had willfully forgotten, that, in the life time of Fulton, they had offered him forty thousand pieces of gold, if he would bring these torpedoes into practice in their own country, that they might use them against the

Gauls,⁹⁶ (with whom they warred continually for more than twenty years): Howbeit they proved faithless to Fulton, and so he did it not for them.

Moreover it came to pass that a certain man, a pilot, even *Joshua*, surnamed *Penny*, became a victim of their spite, because he attempted to go against them with the torpedoes to drive them out of the waters of Columbia.

Now Joshua lived at a place called *East Hampton*, being at the east end of *Long Island*, near *Gardner's Island*, opposite New London.

And the men of Britain came to his house in the night, and stole him away, even out of his bed, and carried him on board a vessel of the king, called the *Ramilies*, from whence he was conveyed to *Halifax* in the province of *Nova Scotia*.

Now while Joshua remained in the dungeons of the king he was treated with the inhospitality of barbarians; moreover, they strove to lead him astray; but he proved faithful to his God and to his country; for he had known the wickedness of Britain in times past.⁹⁷

However, they kept him in bondage many months, after which they suffered him to go to his own country.

For the chief governor of the land of Columbia, and the Great Sanhedrim in their wisdom had ordered two of the servants of the king to be taken and held as hostages for his safe return; and, but for this thing, they would have hanged him, even as a man hangeth a dog.

---

⁹⁶ This was about the time of the Boulogne flotilla.

⁹⁷ Joshua Penny had been, previous to the war, impressed in the British service, and kept in it a number of years.

CHAP. LI.

Affairs in and about New-York, the first commercial city in America—working on the fortifications of Brooklyn and Haerlem— capture of the British tender eagle, by the Yankee smack.

Now, as good sometimes cometh out of evil, so the people of New-York, a great city, which lieth at the mouth of the river Hudson, nigh the sea coast, and containeth more than an hundred thousand souls,

When they beheld the wickedness that was committed by the servants of the king, to the south and round about, began to bestir themselves, and prepare for the dangers with which they were likely to be encompassed:

So it came to pass that the husbandmen from the surrounding country gathered together, and pitched their tents hard by the city.

And the number that came to the defence of the place was about thirty thousand valiant men; moreover there were about five thousand husbandmen from the slate of *New-Jersey*,[98]

Now these men were called *Jersey Blues*, and they were encamped partly at *Paulus Hook*, and partly at a place called the *Narrows*, which lieth to the south of the city about an hundred furlongs, where the destroying engines were placed in multitudes.

---

[98] The exertions of Daniel D. Tompkins, governor of the state of N.York, at this time, will long be remembered by the people.

And when the term of the engagement of these men of Jersey expired, they grieved only that their time was spent for nought; for they were ready and well prepared to meet the servants of the king.

Nevertheless, it was so that the freemen who came to the defence of the city, built strong holds and forts, and raised up fortifications in abundance, inasmuch as the whole place was as it were one camp.

Moreover, on the tenth day of the eighth month, in the eighteen hundred and fourteenth year, the inhabitants assembled together in the midst of the city, even in a place called the *Park*, where the *Federal Hall*, a superb edifice, rears its majestic front; within the walls of which the wise men, the expounders of the law, preside, and deliberate for the benefit of the people.

Now it was about the twelfth hour of the day when the people began to gather themselves together; and, from the porch of the hall, the aged *Willet*, with the star-spangled banner of Columbia waving over his silvery head, addressed the surrounding multitude.

And the people shouted with a loud voice, for the words of his mouth were pleasant to the sons of Liberty, and were in this wise:

Lo! three score and fourteen years have brought with them their bodily infirmities; but were my strength as unimpaired as my love for my country, and that soul which still animates me, ye would not have found me in the rostrum, but in the midst of the battle! fighting against the enemies of freedom.

Thus did he encourage the people to prepare themselves for the protection of the city.

And certain wise men were appointed, by the people; to bring these things into operation.

So the people began to fortify themselves and entrench the high places round about the city.

And when they went out in its defence, to build their strong holds and to raise up their battlements; lo! the steam-boats of *Fulton* conveyed them thither, about a thousand at a time, even towards the heights of *Brooklyn* in the east, and the heights of *Haerlem* in the north.

The young and the old, the rich and the poor, went out together; and took with them their bread and their wine; and cast up the dirt for the defence of the place, freely, and without cost to the state.[99]

And when they went into the boats to cross over the river, there was loud shouting in the boats and on the shore.

Moreover, as they passed along up the Hudson, towards the heights of Haerlem, the fair daughters of Columbia, with hearts glowing with patriotism, waved their lily hands in token of applause.

Likewise, bands of men came from the neighbourhood round about; even from *Newark*, and *Patterson*, and *Paulus Hook*, which lie in the state of *New-Jersey*.

They had also captains appointed over their bands; and *Abraham* and *David* were two among the captains.[100]

Now Abraham, with his band, came a great way, even from the town of Patterson, where the wonderful waterfalls pour headlong over the rocky mountains, reflecting in the sun a thousand brilliant rainbows,

---

[99] The services rendered on this occasion, by that respectable class of citizens, the Firemen of New-York, were particularly conspicuous.

[100] Colonel Godwin and Major Hunt.

Thus for an hundred days did the people of New-York prepare themselves for danger, and cast up entrenchments for many furlongs round about the city; so that the people of Britain were afraid to go against it.[101]

---

[101] So great was the enthusiasm of the people in contributing their personal services to the erection of fortifications on the heights of Haerlem and Brooklyn, that scarcely could an individual be found in the populous city of New-York, from hoary age to tender youth, capable of using a mattock or a spade, who did not volunteer his services in this work of patriotism. Even the Ladies were conspicuous in aiding and cheering the labours of their Fathers, their Husbands, their Brothers, and their Children. Amongst others, the numerous societies of Freemasons joined in a body, and headed by their Grand-Master, who was also Mayor of the city, proceeded to Brooklyn, and assisted very spiritedly in its defence. On this occasion an elderly gentleman, one of the order, who had two sons (his only children) in the service of his country, one of them highly distinguished during the war for his wounds and his bravery, sung the following stanzas, in his own character of Mason and Father, whilst the Lodges were at refreshment:

I.

Hail, Children of Light! whom the Charities send
Where the bloodhounds of Britain are shortly expected;
Who, your country, your wives, your firesides to defend,
On the summit of Brooklyn have ramparts erected:
Firm and true to the trade,
Continue your aid,
Till the top-stone with shouting triumphant is laid;
The free and accepted will never despair,
Led on by their worthy Grand Master and Mayor.

II.

For me, whose dismissal must shortly arrive,
To Heav'n I prefer this my fervent petition:
"May I never America's freedom survive,
"Nor behold her disgrac'd by a shameful submission:
"And, though righteously steel'd,
"If at last she must yield,
"May my sons do their duty, and die in the field:"
But the free and accepted will never despair,
Led on by their worthy Grand Master and Mayor.

Nevertheless the strong ships of war of Britain moved upon the waters of the ocean around the place in numbers, but they were afraid to approach the city; for when they came nigh, the men of Columbia let the destroying engines loose upon them, even those that vomited forth whizzing balls, like shooting stars, red from the fiery furnace.

Notwithstanding, the haughty captains of the ships of Britain would send in their boats to rob the market-men and the fishermen: howbeit, they were sometimes entrapped.

For it came to pass, upon a certain day, that the Poictiers, a mighty ship of the king, lying at a place called *Sandy-Hook*, sent out one of her tenders, even the *Eagle*, in search of this kind of plunder:

Whereupon, a fishing boat of Columbia, called the *Yankee*, under the direction of a chief captain called *Lewis*,[102] prepared herself with a number of men to entrap the Eagle.

So they took a fatted calf, a bleating lamb, and a noisy goose, and placed them upon the deck of the boat; and when the servants of the king came nigh the Yankee, thinking they were about to be treated handsomely with the good things of the land of Columbia, their hearts were rejoiced;

They commanded the vessel called the Yankee to follow after them, towards the ship of the king their master; but at this moment the men of Columbia arose up from their hiding-places in the hold of the boat, and shot into the vessel of Britain.

At the sound of which they were so astonished, that they forgot to put the match to the black dust of the huge howitzer, a destructive engine made of brass, which they had prepared to destroy the men of Columbia.

So they were confused, and surrendered the *Eagle* up to the *Yankee*.

---

[102] Commodore Lewis, commander of the flotilla in the harbor of New-York.

And as they came up to the city, before the *Battery*, which is a beautiful place to the south thereof, the thousands who were assembled there, to celebrate the *Columbian Jubilee*,[103] rent the air with loud shouts of joy, whilst the roaring engines echoed to the skies.

Thus was the lamb preserved, and the proud and cunning men of Britain outwitted with a fatted calf and a Yankee goose.

---

[103] American Independence.

CHAP. LII.

Affairs on the ocean—privateer Prince of Neufchatel—Marquis of Tweedale defeated in Upper Canada—capture of the President —loss of the Sylph—capture of the Cyane and the Levant by the Constitution—capture of the St. Lawrence—capture of the Penguin by the Hornet, Captain Biddle.

Still there was no peace, and the evils of war continued on the face of the deep, and the waters thereof were encrimsoned with the blood of man.

And it came to pass, on the eleventh day of the tenth month, in the eighteen hundred and fourteenth year, that there was a sore battle fought between five barges from the *Endymion*, a strong ship of the king, and a privateer, called the *Prince of Neufchatel*, commanded by the valiant *Ordonneaux*, a man of *Gaul*.

Moreover, the number of the men of Britain were threefold greater than the people of Columbia; and the fight happened nigh a place called *Nantucket*, in the east, journeying towards Boston.

Now they sat their engines to work with dreadful violence; but in about the third part of an hour the barges of the king's ship were overcome; and more than three score and ten of the men of Britain were slain and maimed: the loss in the privateer was six slain, and about a score wounded.

Now this battle happened in the same month in which more than a thousand men of the warriors of Britain, commanded by the *Marquis of*

Tweedale, were defeated at *Black Creek*, in Upper Canada, and driven to their strong holds by the men of Columbia, under the gallant *Bissel*.[104]

Ten days after which the steam frigate, *Fulton the First*, was launched forth into the waters at New-York.

And it came to pass, on the fifteenth day of the first month of the next year, that one of the tall ships of Columbia fell into the hands of the servants of the king;

And she was called the *President*, after the title of the chief magistrate of the land of Columbia; moreover, she was commanded by the gallant Decatur,

Who, but for an accident that befel his ship the day before,[105] whilst he was moving out of the harbor of New-York, would have outsailed the fleet of Britain, and escaped, as did the brave and persevering Hull, of the Constitution, in the first year of the war.[106]

Nevertheless, it was so, that Decatur was, as it were, surrounded by the ships of the king, even five of them; so one of the vessels, called the *Endymion*, fell upon him, and Decatur fought hard against her, and would have taken her;

But the rest of the strong ships came down upon him, and opened their thundering engines, and compelled him to surrender his ship to the fleet of Britain.

However it was a bloody fight; and there fell of the men of Columbia that day twenty and four that were slain outright, and about two score and ten were maimed, after having kept the destroying engines to work about the space of three hours: howbeit, Decatur lost no honor thereby.

---

[104] General Bissel.
[105] She was injured by grounding off the Hook.
[106] Commodore Hull, in this affair, gained much applause, for his manoeuvres in escaping from the British fleet.

Two days after this, a strong vessel of the king, called the *Sylph*, was cast away, in a dreadful storm, at a place called *Southampton*, being on Long Island, where more than an hundred men of Britain perished, in the dead of the night; and the vessel parted asunder and was lost.

Moreover, there were six of the men of Britain who survived their brethren, and were preserved on pieces of the vessel, until the next day, when the neighbouring people took them into their houses and nourished them;

And, when they were sufficiently recovered, that misfortune might not bear too heavy upon them, they were clad, and silver given to them, and they were sent to their own country, at the expense of the people of Columbia.

(Blessed are the merciful, for they shall obtain mercy, saith the scripture.)

Now it came to pass, in these days, whilst the fleets of Britain captured the vessels of Columbia, when they caught them singly upon the ocean, that the single ships of Columbia began to capture the ships of Britain by pairs:

Inasmuch as it happened on the twentieth day of the second month of the same year, that a certain strong vessel called the *Constitution*, commanded by the brave *Stewart*, fell in with two of the strong ships of the king, and compelled them both, in the space of forty minutes, to strike the red cross of Britain to the stars of Columbia.

And the slain and wounded of the king's ships were seventy and seven; of the men of Columbia three were slain and twelve maimed: and the names of the vessels of Britain were the *Cyane* and the *Levant*; but the Levant was retaken in a neutral port,[107] by two strong ships of the king.[108]

---

[107] Porto Prava.
[108] Acasta and Newcastle.

Now the valiant Stewart and his brave men gat great praise for their deeds, even the great Sanhedrim of the people honored them, and gave them twenty thousand pieces of silver.

In the same month the gallant *Boyle*, commanding the privateer *Chasseur*, captured the *St. Lawrence*, a fighting vessel of the king, in the fourth part of an hour.

And the killed and wounded of the St. Lawrence were thirty and eight; and the Chasseur had five slain and eight maimed.

Moreover, it came to pass, on the twenty-third day of the next month, that another fighting vessel of the king, called the *Penguin*, was taken by the *Hornet*, a strong vessel of Columbia, commanded by a man of valor and courage, whose surname was *Biddle*.

However, the battle was a bloody one, and the vessels kept their engines of destruction fiercely in motion, for about the space of half an hour before the flag of Britain was lowered to the stripes of Columbia.

And the slaughter was great; for there fell of the men of Britain two score and one; but the slain of Columbia were only one, and the maimed eleven.

And Biddle was honored greatly for his courage:

However, this was the last sea-fight of importance, being near the close of the war.

Now about this time the navy of Columbia had increased more than fourfold, and the fame thereof had extended to all nations.

For, though Columbia was young, even as it were in the gristle of her youth; yet she now began to resume the appearance, and display the vigor of manhood.

CHAP. LIII.

British fleet arrives near New-Orleans—the American flotilla captured—attacks by the British upon the army of Gen. Jackson.

Now, when the lords and the counsellors, and the wise men of Britain, heard of all the tribulations that befel them in the land of Columbia, they were troubled in their minds.

And as they had made what they called a *demonstration* at Baltimore, they bethought themselves of making another *demonstration* in the south.

(Now the true signification, in the vernacular tongue, of this mighty word demonstration, had always been familiar to the children of Columbia; but the new interpretation, although it wounded the pride of Britain, tickled the sons of Columbia; for, as the world must think to this day, so they could only construe it, an ocular demonstration of British folly.)

So it came to pass, that they gathered together their army and their navy, even two score and ten fighting vessels, carrying therein about twenty thousand men of war; and the name of the chief captain of the navy was Cochrane; and the chief captains of the army were Pakenham, Gibbs, and Keane.

And they essayed to go against the city of *New-Orleans*, which lieth to the south, on the borders of the great river *Mississippi*, in the state of *Louisiana*, which was covenanted, in good faith, to the United States in the days when Jefferson presided as chief governor of the land of Columbia.

But it came to pass, that Jackson, when he had returned from the capture of Pensacola, where he corked up the bottles of iniquity that were ready to be emptied out upon the men of Columbia,

Had arrived with his army at New-Orleans, he began to fortify the place, for he had heard it noised abroad that the king was bent upon taking the city.

About this time, Jackson communed with *Claiborne* the governor, touching the matter; and as his men of war were but few, the valiant husbandmen of Louisiana, Tennessee, Kentucky, and the Mississippi Territory, were informed of the evil, and accordingly they flocked in multitudes to the banners of Jackson.

Now, as Jackson and Claiborne had counted upon the arrival of the strong ships of Britain, so it happened, in the latter part of the eighteen hundred and fourteenth year, that they made their appearance, even in the twelfth month of the year.

And it was so, that when they had come as nigh as they could unto the city with their heavy ships, some of which carried an hundred of the destroying engines, they cast anchor:

And lo, after having passed a certain dangerous place called Pass Christian, they prepared their boats, containing more than a thousand men, and sent them in great numbers against the boats of Columbia that were upon the waters of the lakes about the city.[109]

Now these small vessels of Columbia were commanded by Thomas, a brave man, whose surname was Jones, and he gave them hindrance.

Nevertheless, in the space of about two hours, the boats of Columbia were captured by the vessels of Britain, one after another, until they were all taken:

---

[109] Lakes Borgae and Ponchartrain.

however, the mariners of Columbia fought well, and gained great praise; and the loss of the king was about three hundred.

Now the capture of the gun-boats of the United States upon these waters encouraged the servants of the king, so they began to land their mighty army upon the shores of Columbia in great multitudes from their boats:

And they pitched their tents, and cast up fortifications, and prepared to assail the strong hold of Jackson, the chief captain.

But, that the host of Britain might be discomfited at the onset, Jackson went out with his army against them; but the men of war of the king were twofold greater than the men of Columbia, so Jackson was unable to drive them away.

However, he fought bravely against them, and slew numbers of them; albeit, the slain and maimed of Columbia were about two hundred, so Jackson drew back to his entrenchments, and strengthened himself there.

Now this happened on the twenty and third day of the twelfth month, in the eighteen hundred and fourteenth year.

And it came to pass, on the twenty-seventh day of the same month, that a fighting vessel of the United States, called the *Caroline*, commanded by Daniel, was set fire to, and blown up, by the heated balls of the king's fiery furnace.

On the next day, the whole host of Britain gathered themselves together, and with their might went against the strong hold of Jackson.

But Jackson let the destroying engines loose upon the slaves of Britain, and compelled them to return to their encampments with great loss, even an hundred and two score.

Nevertheless, on the first day of the first month, of the eighteen hundred and fifteenth year, the men of war of Britain came again, and strove to dislodge the army of Jackson; but again they were deceived, and lost about an hundred men.

At this time there arrived to the aid of Jackson about two thousand five hundred valiant men, from the back-woods of Kentucky.

Disappointed in their expectations, and failing in their attempts to discomfit the army of Columbia, the captains and the host of Britain arrayed themselves in their might to go against the hold of Jackson with their whole force.

And the morning of the eighth day of the month was pitched upon, by the men of Britain, for conquering the host of Columbia, and settling themselves in the land of liberty.

So they prepared themselves with their fascines and their scaling ladders, and their bombs and their rockets, and all the weapons of destruction that the ingenuity of Britain could invent.

After which Pakenham, the chief captain of the host of the king, spake to the officers and the men of war that were under him, saying,

Be ye prepared; for, lo! to-morrow, at the dawning of the day, our mighty squadrons shall rush upon these Yankees, and destroy them.

Here will we establish ourselves upon the borders of Columbia; and ye shall be officers, tythe-men, and tax-gatherers, under the king, your master:

Moreover, a day and a night shall ye plunder and riot; and your watch-word shall be, BEAUTY AND BOOTY!

CHAP. LIV.

Grand Battle of New-Orleans.

Now Pakenham, the chief captain of the host of Britain, made an end of addressing the officers and the soldiers of the king:

And it came to pass, in the one thousand eight hundred and fifteenth year of the Christian era, in the first month of the year, and on the eighth day of the month,

Being on the Sabbath day, (which, as it is written in the holy scriptures, Thou shalt REMEMBER AND KEEP HOLY,)

That the mighty army of the king, which had moved out of the strong ships of Britain, came, in their strength, to make conquest of the territory of Columbia, which lieth to the south;

And to place therein a *princely ruler*, and all manner of officers, the servants of the king, even unto a tax-gatherer.

So, early in the morning, they appeared before the camp of the men of Columbia, even the strong hold which Jackson, the chief captain, had fortified.

Their polished steels, of fine workmanship, glittered in the sun, and the movement of their squadrons was as the waving of a wheat-field, when the south wind passeth gently over it.

The fierceness of their coming was as the coming of a thousand untamed lions, which move majestically over the sandy deserts of Arabia.

And the army rested upon the plains of Mac Prardies, nigh unto the cypress swamp, being distant from the city about forty and eight furlongs.

And it was about the rising of the sun, when the battering-rams of the king began to titter their noises; and the sound thereof was terrible as the roaring of lions, or the voice of many thunders.

Moreover, they cast forth bombs, and Congreve rockets, weapons of destruction, which were not known in the days of Jehoshaphat.

Nevertheless, the soul of Jackson failed him not, neither was he dismayed, for he was entrenched round about; and when he raised his hand, he held every man's heart therein.

And Jackson spake, and said unto his captains of fifties, and his captains of hundreds, Fear not; we defend our lives and our liberty, and in that thing the Lord will not forsake us:

Therefore, let every man be upon his watch; and let the destroying engines now utter forth their thunders in abundance:

And ye cunning back-woodsmen, who have known only to hunt the squirrel, the wolf, and the deer, now pour forth your strength Upon the mighty lion, that we may not be overcome.

And as the black dust cast upon a burning coal instantly mounteth into a flame, so was the spirit of the husbandmen of the backwoods of Columbia.

Now the brave men from Tennessee and Kentucky set their shining rifles to work, and the destroying engines began to vomit their thunders upon the servants of the king.

Twice did the host of Britain, in solid columns, come against the entrenchments of Jackson, and twice he drove them back.

Moreover, Daniel the brave, who had raised up defences upon the banks of the river, likewise let his engines loose upon them, and shot into the camp of the king.

And the men of Britain strove to scale the ramparts, and get into the strong hold of Jackson; but the husbandmen drove them back with great slaughter.

The fire and the smoke, and the deafning noise that sounded along the battlements, were tremendous for more than the space of two hours, when the dreadful roarings ceased, for the warriors of the king fled in confusion.

But when the sulphureous vapors arose, behold the battle-ground was covered with the slain and groaning officers and soldiers of the kingdom of Great Britain!

Humanity shuddered at the awful scene, whilst the green fields blushed.

Seven hundred of the servants of the king were slain; and their whole loss that day was two thousand six hundred valiant men, who had fought under Wellington, the champion of England.

And Pakenham, the chief captain of the host of Britain, was amongst the slain; and they served his body as they had served the body of Ross, their chief captain at the Baltimore demonstration, preserving it, in like manner, with the strong waters of Jamaica.

Moreover, one of their chief captains, whose surname was Gibbs, was also slain, and Keane was sorely wounded; so that the charge of the host of Britain that remained from the slaughter, fell to a certain man whose name was Lambert.

The loss of the army of Jackson was *only* seven slain and seven maimed, a circumstance unparalleled in the annals of history: howbeit, there were about two score slain and wounded upon the other side of the river.

Now the whole loss of the king's army, from the time they came against the country of Louisiana until their departure, was about five thousand.

After this they were discouraged, for there was but a faint hope left for them; so they departed, and went into the strong ships of the king, with their chief captain in *high spirits*.

It is written in the book of Solomon, that a fool laugheth at his own folly: now the men of Britain were not inclined to laugh, for they were sorely grieved; and but for the fear of the laughter of others, would have wept outright.

And Jackson, the chief captain of the host of Columbia, gave great praise to the gallant Coffee and Carrol, and Daniel, whose surname was Patterson, and all the valiant men who fought on that glorious day.

Moreover, Jackson was honored with great honor by the people throughout the land of Columbia; even the great Sanhedrim were pleased with him, and exalted his name.

And the inhabitants of New-Orleans were greatly rejoiced, and carried him through the streets of the city above the rest; and the virgins of Columbia strewed his path with roses:

For, lo! he had defended them from the violence of savages, who came in search of *beauty and booty!*

And when the wounded of the host of Britain were brought into the city, the fair daughters of Columbia took their fine linen and bound up the wounds of the poor fainting officers and soldiers of the king, and sat bread and wine before them, to cheer their drooping spirits.

Now again were the servants of the king disappointed; for, as they were sent upon an evil, as well as a foolish errand, they expected not mercy:

And when they saw the goodness that was showered upon them, they said, Surely ye are angels sent down from heaven to heal the wounds inflicted by the folly of nations!

And should we again be led on to battle against your country, with propositions to violate your happiness, our swords, as by magic, shall be stayed, and drop harmless at the feet of VIRTUE and BEAUTY!

CHAP. LV.

Peace.

Now after the fleet of Britain had departed from New-Orleans in dismay, they committed many other depredations of a petty nature.

In the mean time, Cockburn, the wicked, was busily employed in what his heart delighted in; inasmuch as he carried the men of Britain against the borders of South Carolina and Georgia, and continued his system of robbery.

And here, with the strong ships of Britain, he captured a town called *St. Marys*, in the state of Georgia; and, among other evils, he stole away the sable sons of *Ethiopia*,

And conveyed them to the island of Bermuda, of which the king bad made him chief governor, and sold them, after promising them liberty and freedom.

However, it came to pass, about this time, that the news of a peace being made between the nations arrived in the land of Columbia:

For it had happened that the great Sanhedrim, in their wisdom, had sent out *Henry*, surnamed *Clay*, and *Russell*, two wise men, called, in the vernacular tongue, commissioners, to join themselves with Bayard and Gallatin, who were sent before them, to try and make peace:

For the voice of the people of Columbia had spoken peace from the beginning; they wished war might cease, and that the breach between the nations might be healed.

In the mean time the king sent some of his wise men to meet the wise men of Columbia, at a place called *Ghent*, a town a great way off, in the country of *Flanders*:

For it came to pass, that the generous mediation offered by the emperor of Russia was refused by the council of Britain, who had not yielded to the voice of accommodation.

So, when the ministers of the two nations were met, they communed a long time with one another, touching the matter;

But the ministers of Britain raised up difficulties, and demanded certain foolish terms, which, in the Latin tongue, were written *sine qua non*, and which being translated into the *Yankee tongue*, might be said to mean *neck or nothing*.

Nevertheless, in process of time, the wise men of Britain waved their demands, and agreed to the *sine qua non* given to them by the commissioners of Columbia.

So a treaty of peace was made and signed by the commissioners of both parties, on the twenty and fourth day of the twelfth month, of the one thousand eight hundred and fourteenth year of the Christian era.

And the treaty was sent to England, and confirmed by the Prince Regent, on the twenty-eighth day of the same month; for he was tired of the war, and saw no hope of conquering the sons of liberty.

After which it was sent from Britain, across the mighty deep, about three thousand miles, to receive the sanction of the free people of Columbia.

And the great Sanhedrim of the people examined the treaty, and it was accepted and confirmed by them on the seventeenth day of the second month, in the eighteen hundred and fifteenth year.

After which it was signed with the hand-writing of James, the chief governor of the land of Columbia, and published to the world.

Thus was a stop put to the shedding of the blood of man, the noblest work of God; and the noise of the destroying engines sunk down into silence, and every man returned to his own home in peace.

Now when it was known for a certainty that peace was made between the nations, the people throughout the land were rejoiced beyond measure,

(Except the wicked men, who had met at Hartford, and in their folly sent three of their scribes to the chief city, to endeavour to disturb the councils of the great Sanhedrim; which three men, arriving there about this time, were sorely grieved that they and their employers should be held up for a laughing stock to the world; so they sneaked away like men ashamed of their own stupidity.)

And it came to pass, when the news of peace was spread abroad, that the temples of the Lord were opened, and the people of Columbia praised God for his goodness; yea, they thanked him that he had strengthened their arms, and delivered them from the lion's paw

Thus did the children of Columbia praise the Lord in the strength of their youth, and in the days of their prosperity; not waiting till the cold and palsied hand of age had made them feeble, and robbed their prayers of half their virtue.

Henceforth may the nations of the earth learn wisdom: then shall peace become triumphant, and the children of Columbia be at rest;

And, as it is written, their swords may be beaten into ploughshare's, and their spears turned into pruning-hooks.

But, nevertheless, if this war, like all other wars, brought evil upon the sons of men, it demonstrated to the world, that the people of Columbia were able to defend themselves, single-handed, against one of the strongest powers of Europe.

And the mighty kings and potentates of the earth shall learn, from this example of Republican patriotism, that the PEOPLE are the only "*legitimate sovereigns*" of the land of Columbia.

Now the gladness of the hearts of the people of Columbia, at the sound of peace, was extravagant; inasmuch as it caused them to let loose their destroying engines, that were now become harmless, and set in motion their loud pealing bells, that sounded along the splendid arch of heaven.

Moreover, they made great fires and illuminations in the night time, and light was spread over the face of the land;

And the beauty thereof was as if, from the blue and spangled vault of heaven, it had showered diamonds;

And all the nations of the earth beheld the glory of Columbia.

END OF THE HISTORY OF THE LATE WAR.

ALGERINE WAR.

American squadron sails from New-York—arrives on the Mediterranean, and captures the Algerine vessels—treaty of peace with the Dey—affairs at Tunis and Tripoli—Decatur's return to America.

Now it came to pass, that while the war raged between the people of Columbia and the kingdom of Great Britain, other evils rose up in the east.

For the people who inhabited the coast of Barbary. even the Algerines, committed great depredations upon the commerce of Columbia;

Inasmuch as they captured their merchant vessels, and held the men of Columbia who wrought therein in cruel bondage.

Now these Algerines, who were barbarians, dwelt upon the borders of the great sea called the *Mediterranean*, in the way journeying towards the *Garden of Eden*, the cradle of the world; even paradise, where stood the tree of good and evil, and where the great river Euphrates emptieth its waters into the Gulph Persia, which lieth about six thousand six hundred and sixty-six miles to the east of Washington, the chief city of the land of Columbia.

Moreover, the waters of this great sea washed the shores of ancient Palestine, the holy land, the place of our forefathers, and the country of Egypt, where the children of Israel were held in bondage forty years.

Nevertheless, the manifold evils which these barbarians committed, by the instigation of Satan within them, or by being led astray by the enemies of Columbia, raised the voice of the great Sanhedrim against them.

For they had violated the treaty which the people of Columbia had made with them in good faith, and set it at nought.

Now it had curiously happened, that through fear or folly all the nations of the earth had always accustomed themselves to pay tribute to these barbarians;

But the people of Columbia were the first to break the charm, with their brave captains and their destroying engines, many years ago.[110]

Howbeit, they were now again compelled to go against them, and strive to bring them to a sense of justice, if not by persuasion, by communications from the mouths of their destroying engines.

So it came to pass, on the third day of the third month, in the one thousand eight hundred and fifteenth year of the Christian era,

That the great Sanhedrim of the people sent forth a decree, making war upon the people of Algiers, who were ruled by a man whom they called the Dey.

After which, the fleet of Columbia, which had been increased by the folly of Britain, was prepared to go against them; and the gallant Decatur was made chief captain thereof.

The number of the strong vessels was about half a score, and the names of the mightiest amongst them were called the Guerriere, the Macedonian, and the Constellation.

Now the name of the first of these tall ships was after a strong ship of the king of Britain, which was taken by the brave Hull, and burnt upon the waters and the Macedonian was also taken from Britain by. Stephen, sir-named Decatur:

---

[110] Alluding to the war against the Barbary powers, about 1804

And when they came into the waters of Europe, the men of Britain[111] gnashed their teeth with vexation, neither would they behold them, but they turned their backs, for their pride was wounded, whilst the surrounding nations beheld the fleet with astonishment.

Now it was on the eighteenth day of the fifth month, in the same year, in the after part of the day, that the fleet of Columbia spread their wings to the western breeze, and sailed from the haven of New-York;

And, with Decatur, the chief captain, in the Guerriere, they bade farewell to the land of Columbia; and the shouts of the people made the welkin ring, and their blessings followed after them.

And it came to pass, when Decatur, with the fleet of Columbia, arrived in the waters of the Mediterranean sea, being thirty days after he left the land of Columbia,

That he fell in with one of the strongest fighting ships of these barbarians, called the Misoda, and he followed after her, and in less than the space of half an hour, after letting his destroying engines loose upon her, he took her captive, with five hundred men that were in her.

And thirty of the barbarians were slain, among whom was their chief captain, whose name was Rais Hammida, besides many were wounded, and about four hundred prisoners were taken; but Decatur had not a man killed.

Moreover, on the second day afterwards, the fleet of Columbia captured another fighting vessel of the Algerines:

And the slain that were found on board being numbered, were twenty and three, and the prisoners were four score: howbeit, there were none of the

---

[111] At Gibraltar.

people of Columbia even maimed. Thus was the navy of Columbia triumphant in the east, as it had been in the west.

Now these things happened nigh unto a place called Carthagena, on the borders of Spain; and when the Spaniards beheld the skill and prowess of the people of Columbia, they were amazed.

Immediately after this, Decatur departed, and went with his fleet to the port of Algiers, the chief city of the barbarians, lying on the borders of Africa.

But when their ruler beheld the star-spangled banners of Columbia, he trembled as the aspen-leaf; he had heard that his strong vessels were taken by the ships of Columbia, and his admiral slain, and he was ready to bow down.

And Decatur demanded the men of Columbia, without ransom, who were held in bondage; and ten thousand pieces of silver, for the evils they had committed against the people of Columbia: and the Dey had three hours to answer him yea, or nay.

However, he quickly agreed to the propositions of Decatur; and he paid the money, and signed the treaty which Decatur had prepared for him, and delivered up all the men of Columbia whom he held as slaves.

And the treaty was confirmed at Washington, the chief city, and signed by James, the chief governor, on the twenty and sixth day of the twelfth month, in the same year: and Decatur generously made a present of the ship Misoda to the Dey.

Now it came to pass, after Decatur had settled the peace with the Dey of Algiers, according to his wishes, that he sailed against another town of the barbarians, called Tunis.

For the governor of this place, who is called the Bey, had permitted great evils to be committed against the people of Columbia, by the ships of Britain, during the late war; inasmuch as they let them come into their waters, and take away the vessels of Columbia that were prizes.

So, for these depredations, the gallant Decatur demanded forty thousand pieces of silver, which, after a short deliberation, the Bey was fain to grant, lest, peradventure, his city might, from the force of the destroying engines, begin to tumble about his ears.

From the port of Tunis, Decatur departed and went to a place called Tripoli, which lieth to the south thereof, where the brave *Eaton*[112] fought, and erected the banners of Columbia upon the walls of Derne.

Now the chief governor of the Tripolitans, whom they called the *Bashaw*, had suffered like evils to be done by the British in his dominions which had been permitted by the Bey of Tunis.

So likewise, for these evils Decatur demanded thirty thousand pieces of silver, but at first the Bashaw refused to pay it.

However, when he saw the strong ships of Columbia were about to destroy the town, he paid the money, save a little, which he was unable to get, and for which Decatur compelled him to release ten of the captives of other nations, whom he held in bondage.

Thus did Decatur, and his brave men, in the same year, compel the powers of Barbary to respect the banners of Columbia.

Now, having accomplished the object of his expedition, he returned, encircled with glory, to the land of Columbia:

And all the people were rejoiced with great joy, and they made feasts for him, and extolled his name.

---

[112] Geo. Eaton, a hero of the American war with Tripoli some years ago.

Moreover, the great Sanhedrim of the people honored him for his gallant exploits, and gave unto him and his brave officers and mariners, an hundred thousand pieces of silver.

CONCLUSION.

Commodore Bainbridge—Lord Exmouth's Expedition against Algiers.

In the mean time, it had come to pass, that lest the fleet of Decatur should not be sufficient, the great Sanhedrim sent out after him another strong fleet, commanded by the valiant Bainbridge.

But, lo! when his fleet arrived there, the peace had been made, and an end put to the war by the fleet of Decatur: so, after sailing round about the coast, Bainbridge returned home again with the fleet of Columbia.

Now it came to pass, after Decatur had returned in triumph to the land of Columbia, that the lords and the counsellors of Britain became jealous of the fame of Columbia, which she had gained in the east, in releasing her people from slavery, as well as those of other nations.

Moreover, the barbarians committed depredations against the people of Britain, neither did they regard their royal cross, as they did the stars of Columbia.

So the king fitted out a mighty fleet to go against them; and the name of the chief captain thereof was Pellew, to whom the vain people of Britain had given a new name, and had called him lord Exmouth.

Accordingly, as their movements were slow, in the fourth month of the one thousand eight hundred and sixteenth year of the Christian era, the mighty fleet of Britain weighed anchor, and shortly arrived before the city of Algiers, as the fleet of Columbia had done many months before them.

And it was so, that the chief captain of Britain, in the name of the king his master, demanded of the Dey the men of Britain, whom he had held as slaves, and also those of other nations.

But the Dey refused, saying, Ye shall pay unto me five hundred pieces of silver for every slave; then will I release them, and they shall be free.

And Exmouth, the lord of Britain, yielded to the propositions of the barbarians, and accordingly gave unto them the money, even more than twenty horses could draw;

For the number of Christian slaves which Exmouth bought of the barbarians, was about five hundred.

Therefore, the fleet of Britain succeeded not, as did the fleet of Decatur;[113] and the doings of Exmouth might be likened unto a certain mischievous monkey, that, in endeavouring to imitate the shaving of his master's beard, cut his own throat.[114]

Thus, in this thing, did the lords of Britain strive to snatch the laurel from the brow of Columbia:
But her valiant sons had entwined the wreath of glory; and the scribes of this day shall record it, in ever-living characters, on the pyramid of fame.

FINIS.

---

[113] Lord Exmouth narrowly escaped being assassinated while on shore at Algiers.

[114] Lord Exmouth has since, in a second, succeeded in releasing all Christian captives confined in Algiers, and in obtaining the ransom money (to a very considerable amount) which the Dey had previously received from England and Naples.

BIBLE SOCIETIES AND SUNDAY SCHOOLS

It was our intention to have expiated largely on the subject of *Bible Societies*—of their importance, and unprecedented extension throughout Europe and America: but the limits of this publication prevent us from entering far on this subject, luminous as it is; however, in time, another opportunity may offer: at present, the names of the officiating persons in America, being inserted, may serve to show the respectability of this valuable establishment, which posterity will admire.

OFFICERS OF THE AMERICAN BIBLE SOCIETY
PRESIDENT,
Hon. Elias Boudinot, L. I. D. *of New Jersey*
VICE-PRESIDENTS
Hon. JOHN JAY, Esq, of New York.
MATTHEW CLARKSON, Esq. of New York.
DANIEL D. TOMPKINS, Vice-President of the United States.
Hon. DE WITT CLINTON, Governor of the State of New York.
Hon. SMITH THOMPSON, Chief Justice of the State of New York.
Hon. JOHN LANGDON of New-Hampshire.
Hon. CALEB STRONG, of Massachusetts.
Hon. JOHN COTTON SMITH, of Conneticut.
Hon. ANDREW KIRKPATRICK, Chief Justice of the State of New-Jersey.
Hon. WILLIAM TILGHMAN, Chief Justice of the State of Pennsylvania.
Hon. DANIEL MURRAY, of Maryland.
JOSEPH NOURSE, Esq. Register of the Treasury of the United States.
Hon. JOHN QUINCY ADAMS, Secreatry of the State of the United States
FRANCIS S. KEY, Esq. District of Columbia.
Hon. BUSHROD WASHINGTON, of Virginia, Judge of Supreme Court, U.S.
Hon. CHARLES COTESWORTH PINCKNEY, of Charleston, S.C.
His Excellency THOMAS WORTHINGTON, of Ohio.

JOHN BOLTON, Esq, of Georgia.
SECRETARIES.
Rev. John Mason, D.D. Secretary for Foreign Correspondence.
Rev. John B. Romeyen, D.D. Secretary for Domestic Correspondence.
RICHARD VARICK, Esq. Treasurer
Mr. JOHN PINTARD, Recording Secretary and Accountant.
Mr. JOHN E. CALDWELL, Agent

An account of the number of Bible Societies in the United States.

New Hampshire,	1	Virginia,	15
Massachusetts,	14	North Carolina,	2
Vermont,	2	South Carolina,	4
Connecticut,	9	Georgia,	3
New-York,	66	Ohio,	11
New-Jersey,	16	Kentucky,	3
Pennsylvania,	12	Tennessee,	2
Delaware,	2	Louisiana,	1
Maryland,	2	Michigan	1
District of Columbia	1	Missouri,	1

Total Number, 168

The number of these auxiliary societies are rapidly increasing throughout the world, and their good effects may easily be anticipated.—These, and the establishment of *Sunday Schools* in different parts of the United States, has had the most salutary effects, and every good man will no doubt give encouragement to that rich source, which opens a field to virtue, and plants the ever-living seeds of a glorious immortality.

Where wisdom dwells, there virtue reigns,

Note.—For humanity's sake, it is to be hoped, that in future, some, if not all Christian nations joined together, will put an end to the piratical system of these inhuman barbarians.

Note.—The result of the late war has bad the effect of commanding respect from all nations; of which the treatment of the United States frigate Macedonian, captain Warrington, by the Spaniards at Carthagena, (S. A.) from whence she lately arrived, is an instance; for they released the prisoners demanded without hesitation.

COMMERCIAL TREATY.

Whereas a convention between the United States of America and his Britannic Majesty, to regulate the commerce between the territories of the United States and of his Britannic Majesty, was signed at London on the third day of July, in the year one thousand eight hundred and fifteen, by plenipotentiaries respectively appointed for that purpose, which convention is in the words following, to wit:

A CONVENTION,

To regulate the Commerce between the territories of the United States and of his Britannic Majesty.

The United States of America and his Britannic Majesty, being desirous, by a convention, to regulate the commerce and navigation between their respective countries, territories, and people, in such a manner as to render the same reciprocally beneficial and satisfactory, have respectively named plenipotentiaries and given them full powers to treat of and conclude such convention—that is to say the President of the United States, by and with the advice and consent of the Senate thereof, hath appointed for their plenipotentiaries John Quincy Adams, Henry Clay and Albert Gallatin, citizens of the United States; and his Royal highness the Prince Regent, acting in the name and on behalf of his majesty, has named for his plenipotentiaries the right hon. Frederick John Robinson, vice-president of the committee of privy council for trade and plantations, joint paymaster of his majesty's forces, and a member of the Imperial Parliament, Henry Goulburn, esq. a member of the Imperial Parliament, and under secretary of state, and William Adams, esq. doctor of civil laws; and the said plenipotentiaries having mutually produced and shown their said full powers, and exchanged copies of the same, have agreed on and concluded the following articles, videlicet:

ART. I. There shall be between the Territories of the United States of America and all the Territories of His Britannic Majesty in Europe a reciprocal liberty of Commerce. The inhabitants of the two countries respectively shall have liberty freely and securely to come with their ships and cargoes to all such places, ports and rivers in the Territories aforesaid to which other foreigners are permitted to come, to enter into the same, and to remain and reside in any parts of the said Territories respectively, also to hire and occupy houses and warehouses for the purposes of their commerce; and generally the merchants and traders of each nation respectively shall enjoy the most complete protection and security for their commerce, but subject always to the Laws and Statues of the two countries respectively.

ART. II. No higher or other duties shall be imposed on the importation into the United States of any articles, the growth, produce or manufacture of His Britannic Majesty's Territories in Europe, and no higher or other duties shall be imposed on the importation into the Territories of His Britannic Majesty in Europe of any articles the growth, produce or manufacture of the United States, than are or shall be payable on the like articles being the growth, produce, or manufacture of any other foreign country, nor shall any higher or other duties or charges be imposed in either of the two countries, on the exportation of any articles to the United States or to His Britannic Majesty's Territories in Europe, respectively, than such as are payable on the exportation of the like articles to any other foreign country, nor shall any prohibition be imposed on the importation of any articles, the growth, produce, or manufacture of the United States, or of His Britannic Majesty's Territories in Europe, to or from the said territories of his Britannic Majesty in Europe, or to or from the said United States, which shall not equally extend to all other nations.

No higher or other duties or charges shall be imposed in any of the ports of the United States on British vessels, than those payable in the same ports by vessels of the United States; nor in the ports of any of His Britannic Majesty's Territories in Europe on the vessels of the United States, than shall be payable in the same ports on British vessels.

The same duties shall be paid on the importation into the United States of any articles the growth, produce or manufacture of His Britanic Majesty's Territories in Europe, whether such importation shall be in vessels of the United States or in British vessels, and the same duties shall be paid on the importation into the ports of any of his Britannic Majesty's Territories in Europe of any article the growth, produce or manufacture of the United States, whether such importation shall be in British vessels or in vessels of the United States.

The same duties shall be paid and the same bounties allowed on the exportation of any articles, the growth, produce or manufacture of his Britannic Majesty's territories in Europe to the United States, whether such exportation shall be in vessels of the United States or in British vessels; and the same duties shall be paid and the same bounties allowed, on the exportation of any articles, the growth, produce or manufacture of the United States to his Britannic Majesty's territories in Europe, whether such exportation shall be in British vessels or in vessels of the United States.

It is further agreed, that in all cases where drawbacks are or may be allowed upon the re-exportation of any goods, the growth, produce or manufacture of either country, respectively, the amount of the said drawbacks shall be the same, whether the said goods shall have been originally imported in a British or American vessel; but when such re-exportation shall take place from the United States in a British vessel, or from the territories of his Britannic Majesty in Europe in an American vessel, to any other foreign nation, the two contracting parties reserve to themselves, respectively, the right of regulating or diminishing, in such case, the amount of the said drawback.

The intercourse between the United States and his Britannic Majesty's possessions in the West Indies, and on the continent of North America, shall not be affected by any of the provisions of this article, but each party shall remain in the complete possession of its rights, with respect to such an intercourse.

ART. III. His Britannic Majesty agrees that the vessels of the United States of America shall be admitted, and hospitably received, at the principal settlements of the British dominions in the East-Indies, vide-licet, Calcutta, Madras, Bombay, and Prince of Wales' Island, and that the citizens of the said United States may freely carry on trade between the said principal settlements and the said U. States in all articles of which the importation and exportation, respectively, to and from the said territories, shall not be entirely prohibited: provided, only, that it shall not be lawful for them in any time of war, between the British government and any slate or power whatever, to export from the said territories, without the special permission of the British government, any military stores, or naval stores, or rice. The citizens of the U. States shall pay for their vessels, when admitted, no higher or other duty or charge than shall be payable on the vessels of the most favoured European nations, and they shall pay no higher or other duties or charges on the importation or exportation of the cargoes of the said vessels, than shall be payable on the same articles when imported or exported in the vessels of the most favoured European nations.

But it is expressly agreed, that the vessels of the United States shall not carry any articles from the said principal settlements to any port or place, except to some port or place in the United States of America, where the same shall be unladen.

It is also understood, that the permission granted by this article, is not to extend to allow the vessels of the United States to carry on any part of the coasting trade of the said British territories, but the vessels of the United States having, in the first instance, proceeded to one of the said principal settlements of the British dominions in the East-Indies, and then going with their original cargoes, or part thereof, from one of the said principal settlements to another, shall not be considered as carrying on the coasting trade. The vessels of the United States may also touch for refreshment, but not for commerce, in the course of their voyage to or from the British territories in India, or to or from the dominions of the Emperor of China, at the Cape of Good Hope, the Island of St. Helena, or such other places as may be in the possession of Great Britain, in the African or Indian seas, it being well understood that in all that regards this article, the citizens of the United States shall be subject, in all respects, to the laws and regulations of the British government, from time to time established.

ART. IV. It shall be free, for each of the two contracting parties, respectively, to appoint Consuls, for the protection of trade, to reside in the dominions and territories of the other party, but before any consul shall act as such, he shall in the usual form be approved and admitted by the government to which he is sent, and it is hereby declared, that in case of illegal or improper conduct towards the laws or government of the country to which he is sent, such consul may either be punished according to law, if the laws will reach the case, or be sent back, the offended government assigning to the other the reasons for the same.

It is hereby declared that either of the contracting parties, may except from the residence of consuls such particular places as such party shall judge fit to be so excepted.

ART. V. This convention, when the same shall have been duly ratified by the President of the United States, by and with the advice and consent of their Senate, and by his Britannic Majesty, and the respective ratifications mutually exchanged, shall be binding and obligatory on the said United States and his Majesty for four years from the date of its signature, and the ratifications shall be exchanged in six months from this time, or sooner if possible.

Done at London this third day of July, in the year of our Lord one thousand eight hundred and fifteen.

JOHN Q. ADAMS.

H. CLAY.

ALBERT GALLATIN.

FRED. J. ROBINSON.

HENRY GOULBURN. WILLIAM ADAMS.

Now, therefore, be it known, that I, James Madison, President of the United States of America, having seen and considered the forgoing convention, have, by and with the advice and consent of the Senate, accepted, ratified and confirmed the same, and every clause and article thereof, subject to the exception contained in a declaration made by the authority of his Britannic Majesty on the 24th day of November last.

In testimony whereof I have caused the seal of the United States to be hereunto affixed, and have signed the same with my hand. Done at the city of Washington, this twenty-second day of December, A. D. one thousand eight hundred and fifteen, and of the independence of the United States the fortieth.

JAMES MADISON.

By the President.

JAMES MONROE,

Secretary of State.

DECATUR'S TREATY

WITH THE DEY OF ALGIERS.

JAMES MADISON,

PRESIDENT OF THE UNITED STATES OF AMERICA,

To all and singular to whom these presents shall come, greeting:

Whereas a Treaty of Peace and Amity between the United States of America, and His Highness Omar Bashaw, Dey of Algiers, was concluded at Algiers on the thirtieth day of June last, by Stephen Decatur and William Shaler, citizens of the United States, on the part of the United States, and the said Omar Bashaw, Dey of Algiers, and was duly signed and sealed by the said parties, which treaty is in the words following, to wit:

Treaty of peace and amity concluded between the United States of America and His Highness Omar Bashaw, Dey of Algiers.

Article 1. There shall be, from the conclusion of this treaty, a firm, inviolable and universal peace and friendship between the President and the Citizens of the United States of America, on the one part, and the Dey and subjects of the Regency of Algiers in Barbary on the other, made by the free consent of both parties, on the terms of the most favoured nations: and if either party shall hereafter grant to any other nation any particular favor or privilege in navigation or commerce, it shall immediately become common to the other party, freely when it is freely granted to such other nations; but when the grant is conditional, it shall be at the option of the contracting parties to accept, alter, or reject such condition, in such manner as shall be most conducive to their respective interests.

Article 2. It is distinctly understood between the contracting parties, that no tribute, either as biennial presents, or under any other form or name whatever, shall ever be required by the Dey and Regency of Algiers from the United States of America on any pretext whatever.

Article 3. The Dey of Algiers shall cause to be immediately delivered up to the American squadron, now off Algiers, all the American citizens now in his possession, amounting to ten, more or less; and all the subjects of the Dey of Algiers now in possession of the United States, amounting to five hundred, more or less, shall be delivered up to him, the United States, according to the usages of civilized nations, requiring no ransom for the excess of prisoners in their favor.

Article 4. A just and full compensation shall be made by the Dey of Algiers, to such citizens of the United States, as have been captured and detained by Algerine cruisers, or who have been forced to abandon their property in Algiers in violation of the twenty-second article of the treaty of peace and amity, concluded between the United States and the Dey of Algiers on the 5th of September 1795.

And it is agreed between the contracting parties, that in lieu of the above, the Dey of Algiers, shall cause to be delivered forthwith into the hands of the American Consul, residing at Algiers, the whole of a quantity of bales of cotton, left by the late consul general of the United States, in the public Magazines in Algiers, and that he shall pay unto the hands of the said Consul the sum of ten thousand Spanish dollars.

Article 5. If any goods belonging to any nation with which either of the parties are at war, should be loaded on board vessels belonging to the other party, they shall pass free and unmolested, and no attempts shall be made to take or detain them.

Article 6. If any citizens or subjects with their effects belonging to either party shall be found on board a prize vessel taken from an enemy by the other party, such citizens or subjects shall be liberated immediately, and in no case, on any other pretence whatever shall any American citizen be kept in capacity or confinement, or the property of any American citizens found on board of any vessel belonging to any other nation, with which Algiers may be at war, be detained from its lawful owners alter the exhibition of sufficient proofs of American citizenship and of American property by the consul of the United States, residing at Algiers.

Article 7. Proper passports shall immediately be given to the vessels of both the contracting parties, on condition that the vessels of war, belonging to the regency of Algiers, on meeting with merchant vessels belonging to the citizens of the United States of America, shall not be permitted to visit them with more than two persons besides the rowers; these only shall be permitted to go on board without first obtaining leave from the commander of said vessel, who shall compare the passport, and immediately permit said vessel to proceed on her voyage; and should any of the subjects of Algiers insult or molest the commander of any other person on board a vessel so visited, or plunder any of the property contained in her, on complaint being made by the consul of the United States residing in Algiers, and on his producing sufficient proof to substantiate the fact, the commander or Rais of said Algerine ship or vessel of war, as well as the offenders shall be punished in the most exemplary manner.

All vessel of war, belonging to the United States of America, on meeting a cruizer belonging to the regency of Algiers, on having seen her passports and certificates from the consul of the United States, residing in Algiers, shall permit her to proceed on her cruize unmolested, and without detention. No passports shall be granted by either party to any vessels, but such as are absolutely the property of citizens or subjects of the said contracting parties, on any pretence whatever.

Article 8. A citizen or subject of either of the contracting parties, having bought a prize vessel condemned by the other party, or by any other nation, the certificates of condemnation and bill of sale shall be a sufficient passport for such vessel for six months, which, considering the distance between the two countries, is no more than a reasonable time for her to procure proper passports.

Article 9. Vessels of either of the contracting parties patting into the ports of the other, and having need of provisions or other supplies, shall be furnished at the market price; and if any such vessel should so put in from a distance at sea, and have occasion to repair, she shall be at liberty to land, and re-embark her cargo, without paying any customs or duties whatever; but in no case shall she be compelled to land her cargo.

Article 10. Should a vessel of either of the contracting parties be cast on shore within the territories of the other, all proper assistance shall be given to her crew; no pillage shall be allowed. The property shall remain at the disposal of the owners, and if re-shipped on hoard of any vessel for exportation, no customs or duties whatever shall be required to be paid thereon, and the crew shall be protected and succoured, until they can be sent to their own country.

Article 11. If a vessel of either of the contracting parties shall be attacked by an enemy within cannon shot of the forts of the other, she shall be protected as much as is possible. If she be in port, she shall not be seized, or attacked, when it is in the power of the other party to protect her; and, when she proceeds to sea, no enemy shall be permitted to pursue her from the same port, within twenty-four hours after her departure.

Article 12. The commerce between the United States of America and the Regency of Algiers, the protections to be given to merchants, masters of vessels and seamen, the reciprocal rights of establishing consuls in each country, and the privileges, immunities and jurisdictions to be enjoyed by such consuls, are declared to be on the same footing in every respect with the roost favored nations respectively.

Article 13. The consul of the United States of America shall not be responsible for the debts contracted by citizens of his own nation, unless he previously gives written obligations so to do.

Article 14. On a vessel or vessels of war, belonging to the United States, anchoring before the city of Algiers, the consul is to inform the Dey of her arrival, when she shall receive the salutes which are by treaty or custom given to the skips of war Of the most favored nations, on similar occasions, and which shall be returned gun for gun; and if, after such arrival, so announced, any Christians whatsoever, captives in Algiers, make their escape, and take refuge on board any of the ships of war, they shall not be required back again, nor shall the consul of the United States, or commanders of said ships, be required to pay any thing for the said Christians.

Article 15. As the government of the United States of America has in itself no character of enmity against the laws, religion or tranquillity of any nation; and as the said states have never entered into any voluntary war or art of hostility, except in defence of their just rights on the high seas, it is declared by the contracting parties, that no pretext arising from religious opinions shall ever produce an interruption of the harmony existing between the two nations; and the consuls and agents of both nations shall have liberty to celebrate the rites of their respective religions in their own houses.

The consuls respectively shall have liberty and personal security given them to travel within the territories of each other, both by land and sea, and shall not be prevented from going on board any vessels they may think proper to visit; they shall likewise have the liberty to appoint their own drogoman and broker.

Article 16. In case of any dispute arising from the violation of any of the articles of this treaty, no appeal shall be made to arms, nor shall war be declared on any pretext whatever; but if the consul residing at the place where the dispute shall happen, shall not be able to settle the same, the government of that country shall state their grievance in writing, and transmit the same to the government of the other, and the period of three months shall be allowed for answers to be returned, during which time no act of hostility shall be permitted by either party; and in case the grievances are not redressed, and a war should be the event, the consuls, and citizens and subjects of both parties respectively, shall be permitted to embark with their effects unmolested, oh board of what vessel or vessels they shall think proper, reasonable time being allowed for that purpose.

Article 17. If, in the course of events, a war should break out between the two nations, the prisoners captured by either party shall not be made slaves, they shall not be forced to hard labour, or other confinement than such as may be necessary to secure their safe keeping, and shall be exchanged rank for rank; and it is agreed, that prisoners shall be exchanged in twelve months after their capture, and the exchange may be effected by any private individual legally authorised by either of the parties.

Article 18. If any of the Barbary states, or other powers at war with the United States, shall capture any American vessel, and send into any port of the Regency of Algiers, they shall not be permitted to sell her, but shall be forced to depart the port, on procuring the requisite supplies of provisions; but the vessels of war of the United States, with any prizes they may capture from their enemies, shall have liberty to frequent the port of Algiers, for refreshments of any kind, and to sell such prizes in the said ports, without any other customs or duties than such as are customary on ordinary commercial importations.

Article 19. If any of the citizens of the United States, or any persons under their protection, shall have any disputes with each other, the consul shall decide between the parties , and whenever the consul shall require any aid or assistance from the government of Algiers to enforce his decisions, it shall be Immediately granted to him; and if any disputes shall arise between any citizens of the United States and the citizens or subjects of any other nation having a consul or agent in Algiers, such disputes shall be settled by the consuls or agents of the respective nations; and any disputes or suits at law that may take place between any citizens of the United States and the subjects of the Regency of Algiers, shall be decided by the Bey in person, and no other.

Article 20. If a citizen of the United States should kill, wound, or strike a subject of Algiers, or on the contrary, a subject of Algiers should kill, wound, or strike a citizen of the United States, the law of the country shall take place, and equal justice shall be rendered, the consul assisting at the trial; but the sentence of punishment against an American citizen shall not be greater, or more severe, than it would be against a Turk in the same predicament; and if any delinquent should make his escape, the consul shall not be responsible for him in any manner whatever.

Article 21. The consul of the United States of America shall not be required to pay any customs or duties whatever on any thing be imports from a foreign country for the use of his house and family.

Article 22. Should any of the citizens of the United States of America die within the limits of the Regency of Algiers, the Dey and his subjects shall not interfere with the property of the deceased, but it shall be under the immediate direction of the consul, unless otherwise disposed of by will. Should there be no consul, the effects shall be deposited in the hands of some person worthy of trust, until, the party shall appear who has a right to demand them, when they shall render an account of the property; neither shall the Dey or his subjects give hindrance in the execution of any will that may appear.

Now therefore be it known, That I, JAMES MADISON, President of the United States of America, having seen and considered the said Treaty, have, by and with the advice and consent of the Senate, accepted, ratified and confirmed the same, and every clause and article thereof.

In testimony whereof, I have caused the seal of the United States to be hereunto affixed, and have signed the (L. S.) same with my hand. Done at the city of Washington—this twenty-sixth day of December, A. D. one thousand eight hundred and fifteen, and of the Independence of the United States the fortieth.

JAMES MADISON.

By the President,

JAMES MONROE, Secretary of State.

ARTICLES OF AGREEMENT.

Between the United States of America and the Creek Nation.

JAMES MADISON,

President of the United States of America.

To all and singular to whom these presents shall come, Greeting:

WHEREAS certain articles of agreement and capitulation were made and concluded on the ninth day of August, in the year of our Lord one thousand eight hundred and fourteen, between Major General Andrew Jackson, in the name of the President of the United States of America, for and in behalf of the said United States, and the chiefs, deputies, and warriors, of the Creek Nation; and whereas the President having seen and considered the same, and, by and with the advice and consent of the Senate of the United States, duly ratified and confirmed the said articles of agreement and capitulation, which are in the words following to wit:

Articles of agreement and capitulation, made and concluded this ninth day of August, one thousand eight hundred and fourteen, between major general Andrew Jackson, on behalf of the President of the United States of America, and the chiefs, deputies, and warriors of the Creek Nation.

WHEREAS an unprovoked, inhuman, and sanguinary war, waged by the hostile Creeks against the United States, hath been repelled, prosecuted and determined, successfully, on the part of the said States, in conformity with principles of national justice and honorable warfare—And whereas consideration is due to the rectitude of proceeding dictated by instructions relating to the re-establishment of peace: Be it remembered, that prior to the conquest of that part of the Creek nation hostile to the United States, numberless aggressions had been committed against the peace, the property, and the lives of citizens of the United States, and those of the Creek nation in amity with her, at the mouth of Duck river, Fort Mimms, and elsewhere, contrary to national faith, and the regard due to an article of the treaty concluded at New-York, in the year seventeen hundred ninety, between the two nations : That the United States, previously to the perpetration of such outrages, did, in order to ensure future amity and concord between the Creek nation and the said states, in conformity with the stipulations of former treaties, fulfil, with punctuality and good faith, her engagements to the said nation: that more than two-thirds of the whole number of chiefs and warriors of the Creek nation, disregarding the genuine spirit of existing treaties, suffered themselves to be. instigated to violations of their national honor, and the respect due to a part of their own nation faithful to the United States and the principles of humanity, by impostors denominating themselves Prophets, and by the duplicity and misrepresentation of foreign emissaries, whose governments are at war, open or understood, with the United States. Wherefore,

First—The United States demand an equivalent for all expenses incurred in prosecuting the war to its termination, by a cession of all the territory belonging to the Creek nation within the territories of the United States, lying west, south, and south-eastwardly, of a line to be run and described by persons duly authorised and appointed by the President of the United States— Beginning at a point on the eastern bank of the Coosa river, where the south boundary line of the Cherokee nation crosses the same; running from thence down the said Coosa river with its eastern bank according to its various meanders to a point one mile above the mouth of Cedar creek, at Fort Williams, thence east two miles, thence south two miles, thence west to the eastern bank of the said Coosa river, thence down the eastern hank thereof according to its various meanders to a point opposite the upper end of the great falls, (called by the natives Woetumka) thence east from a true meridian line to a point due north of the mouth of Ofucshee, thence south by a like meridian line to the mouth of Ofucshee on the south side of the Tallapoosa river, thence up the same, according to its various meanders, to a point where a direct course will cross the same at the distance of ten miles from the mouth thereof, thence a direct line to the mouth of Summochico creek, which empties into the Chatahouchie river on the east side thereof below the Eufaulau town, thence east from a true meridian line to a point which shall intersect the line now dividing the lands claimed by the said Creek nation from those claimed and owned by the state of Georgia: Provided, nevertheless, that where and possession of any chief or warrior of the Creek nation, who shall have been friendly to the United States during the war, and taken an active part therein, shall be within the territory ceded by these articles to the United States, every such person shall be entitled to a reservation of land within the said territory of one mile square, to include his improvements as near the centre thereof as may be, which shall insure to the said chief or warrior, and his descendants, so long as he or they shall continue to occupy the same, who shall be protected by and subject to the laws of the United States; but upon the voluntary abandonnent thereof, by such possessor or his descendants, the right of occupancy or possession of said land, shall devolve to the United States, and be identified with the right of property ceded hereby.

Second—The United States will guarantee to the Creek nation, the integrity of all their territory eastwardly and northwardly of the said line to be run and described as mentioned in the first article.

Third—The United States demand, that the Creek nation abandon all communication, and cease to hold any intercourse with any British or Spanish post, garrison, or towns; and that they shall not admit among them, any agent or trader, who shall not derive authority to hold commercial, or other intercourse with them, by license from the President or authorised agent of the United States.

Fourth—The United States demand an acknowledgment of the right to establish military posts and trading houses, and to open roads within the territory, guarranteed to the Creek nation by the second article, and a right to the free navigation of all its waters.

Fifth—The United States demand, that a surrender be immediately made, of all the persons and property, taken from the citizens of the United States, the friendly part of the Creek nation, the Cherokee, Chickesaw, and Choctaw nations, to the respective owners; and the United States will cause to be immediately restored to the formerly hostile Creeks, all the property taken from them since their submission, either by the United States, or by any Indian nation in amity with the United States, together with all the prisoners taken from them during the war.

Sixth—The United States demand the caption and surrender of all the prophets and instigators of the war, whether foreigners or natives, who have not submitted to the arms of the United States, and become parties to these articles of capitulation, if ever they shall be found within the territory guaranteed to the Creek nation by the second article.

Seventh—The Creek nation being reduced to extreme wants and not at present having the means of subsistence, the United States, from motives of humanity, will continue to furnish gratuitously the necessaries of life, until the crops of corn can be considered competent to yield the nation a supply, and will establish trading houses in the nation, at the discretion of the President of the United States, and at such places as be shall direct, to enable the nation, by industry and economy, to procure clothing.

Eighth—A permanent peace shall ensue from the date of these presents forever, between the Creek nation and the United States, and between the Creek nation and the Cherokee, Chickesaw, and Choctaw nations.

Ninth—If in running east from the mouth of Summochico creek, it shall so happen that the settlement of the Kennards, fall within the lines of the territory hereby ceded, then, and in that case, the line shall be run east in a true meridian to Kitchofoonee creek, thence down the middle of said creek to its junction with Flint River, immediately below the Oakmulgee town, thence up the middle of Flint river to a point due east of that at which the above line struck the Kitchofoonee creek, thence east to the old line herein before mentioned, to wit: the line dividing the lands claimed by the Creek nation, from those claimed and owned by the state of Georgia.

The parties to these presents, after due consideration for themselves and their constituents, agree, to ratify and confirm the preceding articles, and constitute them the basis of a permanent peace between the two nations; and they do hereby solemnly bind themselves, and all the parties concerned and interested, to a faithful performance of every stipulation contained therein. In testimony whereof, they have hereunto interchangeably set their hands and affixed their seals, the day and date above written.

ANDREW JACKSON,
Maj. Gen. Commanding 7th Military District.

Done at Fort Jackson, in presence of

CHARLES CASSEDY, Acting Secretary.

BEN J. HAWKINS, Agent for Indian Affairs.

RETURN J. MEIGS, A. C. Nation.

ROBERT BUTLER, Adjutant Gen. United States* Army.

J. C. WARREN, Assistant Agent for Indian Affairs.

Tustunnuggee X Thlucco, Speaker of the Upper Creeks L. S.

Tustunnuggee X Hoppoiee, Speaker of the Lower Creeks L.S.

(Signed by thirty-four other chiefs, omitted here.)

GEO. MAYFIELD. }

ALEX. CORNELS, } Public Interpreters.

GEO. LOVETT, }

Now, therefore, to the end that the said articles of agreement and capitulation may be observed and performed with good faith on the part of the United States, I, James Madison, President of the United States of America aforesaid, have caused the premises to be made public, and do hereby enjoin and require all persons bearing office, civil or military, within the said United States, and all others, citizens or inhabitants thereof, or being within the same ; faithfully to observe and fulfil the said articles of agreement and capitulation, and every clause and provision thereof.

In testimony whereof, I have caused the seal of the (SEAL) United States to be affixed to these presents, and signed the same with my hand.

Done at the city of Washington, the sixteenth day of February, in the year of our Lord one thousand eight hundred and fifteen, and of the sovereignty and independence of the United States the thirty ninth.

JAMES MADISON.

By the President,

JAMES MONROE,

Acting Secretary of State,

ERATA.

Page 94. verse 13, read "the vessel of the king was captured."

Page 106. verse 54 should read thus: "And Henry, the chief captain, gave great honor to the captains under him, even Ripley, Forsyth and Euslis, and all the brave men that fought that day."

Page 278.—For "Major Goodwin" read Colonel Godwin."

LITERARY AND COMMERCIAL.

D. Longworth is about re-publishing from a superb London edition, Travels in Russia and Poland, by Robert Johnston, to be comprised in one octavo vol. The generous offer of the Emperor of Russia to become a mediator, between the United States and Great Britain, not only exhibits in striking colors his humanity, but as Great Britain refused the offer, must naturally interest the American people in his behalf. There is no doubt but a more intimate acquaintance with Russia and its resources, would be an object worthy the attention of commercial men In America. And the information contained in this work will be found particularly important to the commercial interest of the United States.—To the scholar, the historian, and the philosopher it will be a delicate repast. If this were not believed to be the fact, this paragraph should not have intruded itself here.

www.ingramcontent.com/pod-product-compliance
Lightning Source LLC
Chambersburg PA
CBHW020419010526
44118CB00010B/327